THE *SPHOṬA* THEORY OF LANGUAGE

The *Sphoṭa* Theory of Language

A Philosophical Analysis

Harold G. Coward

MOTILAL BANARSIDASS PUBLISHERS
PRIVATE LIMITED • DELHI

First Edition: Delhi, 1980
Reprint: Delhi, 1986, 1997

ISBN: 81-208-0181-4

Also available at:

MOTILAL BANARSIDASS
41 U.A. Bungalow Road, Jawahar Nagar, Delhi 110 007
8, Mahalaxmi Chamber, Warden Road, Mumbai 400 026
120 Royapettah High Road, Mylapore, Madras 600 004
Sanas Plaza, Subhash Nagar, Pune 411 002
16 St. Mark's Road, Bangalore 560 001
8 Camac Street, Calcutta 700 017
Ashok Rajpath, Patna 800 004
Chowk, Varanasi 221 001

PRINTED IN INDIA
BY JAINENDRA PRAKASH JAIN AT SHRI JAINENDRA PRESS,
A-45 NARAINA, PHASE I, NEW DELHI 110 028
AND PUBLISHED BY NARENDRA PRAKASH JAIN FOR
MOTILAL BANARSIDASS PUBLISHERS PRIVATE LIMITED,
BUNGALOW ROAD, DELHI 110 007

To Professor T. R. V. MURTI

FOREWORD

We live, move and have our being in language. Even to criticize its faults and limitation, to the extent of negating it, we have to use language. Language is not an accidental accretion to thought, but its very essence. As Bhartṛhari says: There is no cognition without the operation of words; all cognition is shot through and through by the word. All knowledge is illumined through the word (*śabdena bhāsate*) *na so'sti pratyayo loke yaḥ śabdānugamād ṛte| anuviddham iva jñānaṁ sarvaṁ śabdena bhāsate || Vākyapadiya* I, 115(123) Dr. Cowrad quotes the opening verses from St. John's Gospel: "In the beginning was the Word, and the Word was with God, and the Word was God." This brings out its universality and fundamental basis of all life and thought—its divinity.

When a speaker makes use of identical and repeatable words, (say sounds), to convey some meaning, something not present on the scene; and when this is understood by the hearer, language functions. In this sense, even animals (dogs, horses and elephants, for instance) understand and obey commands, and one 'talks' to them. Indian speculations on language began with the Veda and have continued till recently without any break. In the *Ṛgveda* several hymns are devoted to *Vāk* (Speech) and the same spiritual trends are continued in the *Brāhmaṇas* and the *Upaniṣads*. Patañjali in his *Mahābhāṣya* quotes some of these striking utterances and comments on them. It can truly be said that the philosophy of language as cultivated by the school of Grammar and the Mīmāṁsā is the elaboration of the suggestions found in the Veda. The divine nature of speech, rather its being the great God himself, the creative and illuminative power of the word, and the different levels of speech—these doctrines which formed the main plank of the philosophy of language in Indian thought,—all stem from the Veda. The ancillary disciplines of the Veda, phonetics (*Śikṣā*), grammar (*Vyākaraṇa* language analysis) and *Nirukta* (definitions of terms) were directly connected with the Veda. The Mīmāṁsā is basically a systematic exegesis of Vedic texts. On this arena of language, the different philosophical systems met and clashed. It is no exaggeration to say that Indian philosophy is repeated twice over—once in the accredited metaphysical systems as we know them and, once again, in their standpoint with regard to language. Almost all types of metaphysics—Absolutism and Pluralism, Empiricism and Transcendentalism, Realism and Nominalism and their shades and sub-shades are found here. Every system of philosophy had to consider language at some stage or other, and each one had to ponder over ultimate questions concerning the relation of the word to reality, of the modes of meaning and the validity of Verbal Knowledge (*Śabda-Pramāṇa*). Their metaphysical bias determined their answers to these questions. It should be an interesting and almost an engrossing study to view and expound Indian Philosophy from this angle. If the Greeks built their science and philosophy and culture on mathematics, especially geometry, the Indians built theirs on Language (*Śabda-Śāstra*). It is the exemplar of all disciplined investigations.

Two principal schools—the Mīmāṁsā and Philosophy of Grammar-made massive and most significant contributions to the philosophy of language, with Nyāya playing an important role on the empirical level. The Ālaṁkārikas (Rhetoricians) also made very acute analyses of linguistic and literary meaning. We may re-interpret Indian philosophy as stemming from two principal traditions based on their different evaluations of language. The Brahmanical tradition stemming from the Veda takes language as of Divine Origin (*Daivī Vāk*), as Spirit descending and embodying itself in phenomena, assuming various guises and disclosing its real nature to the sensitive soul. The well-known *Ṛgveda* verse, (*catvāri śṛṅgā trayo asya pādā dve śirṣe sapta hastāso asya/ tridhā baddho vṛṣabho roravīti mahādevo martyām ā viveśa* // (*Ṛgveda,* 4.58.3) expresses this truth in poetic form. It symbolises Speech as the Bellowing Bull of abundant fecundity, as the Great God descending into the world of mortals. Patañjali asks: 'Who is this Great God' and answers, 'Speech itself' (*mahān devaḥ śabdaḥ*). Another verse of the *Ṛgveda* (quoted by Coward) tells us that the ignorant man seeing and hearing speech in its overt manifest forms does not know its real nature. To the wise, Speech reveals her intrinsic nature, even as the loving wife does to her husband. The Vedānta,

Mīmāṁsā, the Sāṁkhya-Yoga and the School of Grammar and Kashmir Śaivism, among several others, are loyal to this tradition.

In opposition to this high evaluation of language, we have the naturalistic conception of language, as an arbitrary and conventional tool. This stand denied the validity of Verbal Testimony as a valid source of knowledge. It was nominalistic, positivistic and sceptical in this regard. The Cārvāka and schools of Buddhism, including the Mādhyamika, are representatives of this tradition. Empiricists as they are, the Jaina and the Nyāya-Vaiśeṣika occupy a somewhat intermediary position. Dr. Coward in his book makes pointed reference to this two-fold tradition and adequately analyses their stand (pp. 17-18 ff, 49 ff.)

That language is underived and the word is a form and is thus distinct from its material embodiment, sound (*dhvani*), are established by the theory of the Eternality of the Word (*Śabda-nityatvavāda*) both by the Mīmāṁsā and the Grammar School. Words and their relation with meaning are eternal and underived and impersonal. It may be thought that we give names to persons and things and thus initiate new conventions, and that the same logic should be applied to the other words also (common words). They too were the result of convention (*saṅketa*), and where human convention is not available, recourse may be had to divine convention. Against this view, the Mīmāṁsā argues rightly that the relation between the word and the meaning is not an arbitrary convention, established by man or even by God either now or in the past. We do not have record of any such convention. Convention itself presupposes language, which is sought to be derived from Convention. To make convention, words have to be used and understood by persons participating in the convention. This is clearly circular. Invoking God does not help here. How could God make known his intentions, his conventions between particular words and their specific meanings, to persons who did not use language already; there would be a communication-gap. And if men were already using language, God's convention does not obviously initiate language as claimed. However far back we might push the beginning of convention, we would still find language use preceding it. An absolute beginning of language is untenable. Linguistic usage is continuous.

What constitutes the unit of language? Does each letter of a word or each word in a sentence have a separate meaning by itself or do they have meaning as combined together. Obviously, not the first alternative, for each letter of any particular word does not convey either a part or the whole meaning. Nor the second; for, combination of syllables which makes up the word or the several words which make up the sentence are not present in consciousness as one whole. Notoriously, the syllables of a word nor the several words which are supposed to constitute a sentence are never together; they die out as they are pronounced. And, when we arrive at the last letter of a word or the last word of a sentence, the previous elements have already dropped out. How then is a combination possible? It may be pointed out, as is done by the Mīmāṁsaka and the Nyāya philosophers, that we have the last word or rather the last phoneme (letter, *antima-varṇa*) actually present in our ken and this actual perceptual state, combined with the memory (*smaraṇa*) of the other letters and words or their traces (*saṁs-kāras*) engenders the meaning as a whole. But order or sequence of letters and words should also be taken into account; otherwise, the words 'Lamp' and 'Palm' would have the same meaning. But what would determine the order of words in the absence of an awareness of the whole. It must be pointed out here that on the Mīmāṁsā or Nyāya hypothesis a Whole Word or a Whole Sentence can never be present in our consciousness. Again, as the meaning is a whole, a unit, and is understood as a whole or one unit, the verbal condition which engenders the one meaning must likewise be a whole. The Grammar School is led, from such considerations, to advance the Doctrine of Sphoṭa—the Unitary Whole Word particularly the *Akhaṇḍa-Vākyārtha-Sphoṭa*—that the sentence is an indivisible unit whole. And this engenders meaning. The separate letters or the words serve merely to manifest (abhivyañjanā) bring the *Akhaṇḍa-Vākya-Sphoṭa* into play. That is the several sounds of letters and words (the *dhvani*) uttered by the speaker and heard by the hearer serve merely the purpose of arousing or invoking the *Sphoṭa* (Whole Sentence Unit) already present in each one of us. Verbal communication is made possible, because of the identical and eternal *Sphoṭa* equally and fully present in both the speaker and the hearer, in every one of us. The physical and physiological sounds, uttered in a sequence and heard at the other end by the hearer, only serve to manifest the Eternal Word already present.

It may be rebutted, as is done by the Mīmāṁsā and Nyāya, that the manifestation or invoking of the *Sphoṭa* does not escape the objections raised against the theory of individual letters or separate words generating meaning. Is the *Sphoṭa* manifested by a few letters or by all the letters taken together and in what order? In any case, the letters or the words of a sentence are indispensable, although the Grammarian belittles their function and thinks little of them. In addition, the Grammar School makes a gratuitous assumption of a mythical and superfluous entity like the Sphoṭa.

This criticism misses the deeper significance of the *Sphoṭa* conception. In linguistic apprehension, as in other cognitions, there is the interplay of two factors of two different levels—the empirical manifold of sense-data (the separate letters or words uttered by the speaker and heard by the hearer, the overt sounds or words in common parlance) and the transcendental or *a priori* synthesis of the manifold by the Category of the Whole Unit Word which alone imparts a unity and singleness of purpose to those empirical elements which would otherwise have remained a mere manifold, unorganised without unity. The *Sphoṭa* is the Real Sentence or Word-Unit which operates behind the facade of the overtly sensuous syllables and words. Against the empiricism of the Mīmāṁsā and the Nyāya, the Grammar School is a form of Transcendentalism. Epistemologically, it is a two-level theory as applied to linguistic cognition. The Advaita Vedānta also states that in all Cognition Brahman or the Self-Luminous Consciousness (*Svaprakāśa Caitanya*) is identically present and is made manifest. When we are perceiving the pot or the table, the Vedānta holds that we are really perceiving *Brahman* (the Unitary Whole, Undivided Consciousness) as seemingly delimited by the pot or the table, which are floating and adventitious adjectives of the Universal Substantive, *Brahman*. The Vedānta is also committed to a Two-Level Theory on the epistemic plane. These two factors, *Sphoṭa* and the empirical Sounds which manifest it belong to two different orders—one is empirical and the other is submerged and hidden and has therefore to be excited and manifested by the overt sounds (*nādābhivyaṅgyaḥ sphoṭaḥ*), but is really the basis or reality of the empirical.

The battle royal is between the Grammar School on the one hand and the Mīmāṁsā (as represented by Kumārila Bhaṭṭa principally and the Nyāya as represented by Vācaspati Miśra, Jayanta Bhaṭṭa and others. The arguments and counter-arguments put forth by both sides are explained and presented with great skill, clarity and understanding by Dr. Coward. Maṇḍana Miśra in his *Sphoṭa-siddhi* states the Grammarian's position and refutes with rigour and cogency the Mīmāṁsā arguments. The sustained argumentations and level of sophistication exhibited evoke one's wonder. This constitutes one of the very brilliant portions of the *Sphoṭa Theory of Language* (Chapter 6).

We have seen that the Grammar School, like the Advaita Vedānta, is committed to Levels of Language and is based on an absolutism. As Dr. Coward puts it: "If one develops the *Sphoṭa* position purely in terms of logical consistency, a monistic hierarchy such as the following necessarily results. Just as the phonemes are only unreal abstractions of the word, so also words are unreal abstractions of the sentence and the sentences unreal abstractions of the paragraph. Even the paragraph is not the ultimate unity, since it is only an unreal division of the chapter of the book. At the top of this language hierarchy perhaps there is only one indivisible reality within our literary self, which, due to our human ignorance, or limitation or avidyā, can only manifest itself in such unreal forms as the book, the chapter, the paragraph, the sentence and the word. The underlying principle, maintains Bhartṛhari, is that all difference presupposes a unity (*abheda-purvako hi bhedaḥ*). Where there is difference or parts there must be an underlying identity, otherwise, the one could not be related to the other end and each would constitute a world by itself. This is the grounding for Bhartṛhari's metaphysical speculation. Our manifestation of one central, eternal and indivisible principle—*Śabda Brahman* or *Parā Vāk*, having the *Praṇava* as its mystic unitary utterance." (Chapter 6, p. 119, note 2).

For the Grammar School the divisions of Words and Letters

is convenient fiction made for pedagogical purposes, to teach words with precision and great economy of effort. As Bhartṛhari says: *Śāstraiḥ prakriyābhedaiḥ avidyaivopavarṇyate* meaning that the various technical procedures adopted in the Treatises teach only forms of false appearances (*avidyā eva upavarṇyate*). For instance take the word *Bhavati* (Third person singular form of present tense of the verb root *bhū, sattāyām*) is derived by Pāṇini by taking *Bhū* as the Verb root ("to be", to become, to be present etc.) and adding the suffix *ti* (*p*) along with an intermediary 'a' (*śap*) and changing the root *bhū* into *bho*, etc. Instead, we can say the verb root is *bhava* and the suffix is *ti*. But how then are we to account for the past participle of *bhū* which is *bhūta, bhūtavān* and other noun forms as *bhūti* etc. We can say that in such cases *bhava* gets a vowel change (*saṃprasāraṇa*) etc. All this is to show that there is nothing sacrosanct about the Pāṇinean techniques and processes. The only criterion is that with how fewer steps and processes we could acquire the greatest amount of words, the law of parsimony and economy of effort. The basic division of sentences into words and words into bases (nouns and verb-roots) with their respective suffixes (*prakṛti-pratyaya-vibhāga*) on which the whole science of Grammar is based is itself phenomenal, not real; it is a convenient fiction to manipulate and handle words with precision and ease.

As the Grammarians say that they, in all simplicity and exhuberance, began with the investigation of words, how to manipulate and acquire them. They began with the systematic study of overt speech. Lo ! they stumbled upon the WORD-ABSOLUTE (*Śabda-Brahman*), like a person engaged upon picking up straw and little faggots stumbling upon a big diamond. The divisions of the levels of Speech into Vaikharī (Overt Speech, Usage of SOUNDS), Madhyamā (Internal Speech or *antarjalpa*) where there is the order or sequence of words and meanings, and this is preceded logically by a more unitary stage where there is no order or sequence of words, but just a glimpse of the separation of word and meaning, the stage of *intentionality* or the primordial urge to express oneself. This stage is called *paśyanti*, the onward or forward-looking phase. As in this stage there is the distinction between Word and Meaning (*Śabda* and *artha*), it presupposes a Unitary

Ground on which this distinction is super-imposed. As we have seen, Bhartṛhari subscribes to the principle that wherever there are differences and distinctions, there is a basic unity underlying these differences, for otherwise these differences could not be related and will fall asunder. Each difference could become a radical monad; we cannot even assert there are other monads, for this requires a relation and unification, which monadism utterly denies. So Bhartṛhari is logically led to the *Parā Vāk* or *Brahman* (*Śabda-Brahman*) as the Ultimate Reality from which the World has originated. He calls it *Śabda-Brahman* because the approach to the Highest is made here through the Word (*Śabda*) or Analysis of Language or because It is expressed through the words. Bhartṛhari begins his great treatise, *Vākyapadiya*, with key-note Verse: The Word Reality (*Śabda-Tattvam*), without beginning or end, the Immutable Word (*akṣaram*) appears (*vivartate*) as meaning and thing (*arthabhāvena*); thus happens the World-Process (*prakriyā jagato yataḥ*). This verse has to be construed in an absolutistic sense, as the whole trend and teaching of the *Vākyapadiya* would show.

The Philosophical Analysis of Language is not just a logical exercise, to satisfy intellectual curiosity, but an earnest and sustained spiritual approach to identify oneself with the Basic Ground of Word Phenomena, with *Śabda-Brahman*. Bhartṛhari elaborates this approach as *Śabda-yoga* or *Śabdapūrvaka-yoga*, and in this sense Grammar is a Straight Pathway to Freedom (*mokṣamāṇānām ajihmā rājapaddhatiḥ*). Dr. Coward deals with this aspect of the Sphoṭa philosophy of Language.

Dr. Coward has accomplished his study of the Sphoṭa Theory of Language with discerning scholarship, authenticity and commendable philosophical acumen. He could see things from within, as by his sympathy he could identify himself with the attitude of the *Sphoṭa* school. This has enabled him to appreciate the inherent strength and depth of the Grammarian's standpoint. Of course, the arguments and counter-arguments of the *Sphoṭa* theory and its Opponents do not lead to the absolute rejection or negation of any standpoint. No system of philosophy has refuted or knocked out other positions, in spite of the heroic words used by the disputants. The discussion and the dialectic serve to bring out the basic philosophical standpoints and clarifies their implicit differences. One may not accept the *Sphoṭa Theory*, if he is not inclined metaphysically to do so. But one is bound to appreciate the basic principles underlying the Sphoṭa Theory and the spiritual Intuition behind it. I have no manner of doubt that Dr. Coward's book would prove of immense value in understanding with insight the *Sphoṭa* theory and many other problems in the philosophy of language.

Banaras Hindu University,
Varanasi.

T. R. V. MURTI

PREFACE

My interest in Sphoṭa Theory came about in a strange but fitting way. For several years as a student of Western Psychology and Religion I had been fascinated with the question "How do we know via language?" How do the ordinary words of everyday conversation, the poetic words of aesthetic experience, and the special words of scriptural revelation convey their meaning and truth to us? In Western philosophy, psychology, and theology, I found this study very difficult to pursue because of the academic alienation that exists among these disciplines.

One day, while feeling depressed and discouraged at the lack of progress I was making in this study using Western sources, I encountered Professor T. R. V. Murti. Professor Murti asked me what the problem was. I told him, and he explained to me that just that topic had been given detailed study in Indian thought for three thousand years or more. He invited me to become his student and to pursue the study of language and revelation in the Indian context. This event marked a significant turning point in my life and my studies. Working under Professor Murti's guidance I found that in traditional Indian thought there were no brick walls between disciplines and that the question of how language conveys and reveals word meanings had a long and respected academic parentage. Professor Murti introduced me to the ancient debate between Kumârila Bhaṭṭa, the Mîmâṁsaka and Bhartṛhari the great Grammarian. I found myself particularly drawn to Bhartṛhari's Sphoṭa Theory because it provided an explanation as to how language functions that made sense philosophically, theologically, and seemed to have a sound psychological basis. Sphoṭa Theory also seemed to relate in a creative way both to very ancient Western concepts of language, such as Plato's notion of eternally existing ideas and the *logos* conception in the Gospel of John, as well as to some very modern notions, such as Chomsky's theory of innate universal grammatical structures.

This book presents the results of my philosophical analysis of Sphoṭa Theory. I have also engaged in a psychological study but those findings will form the contents of a separate volume to be published later. In addition to my teacher, Professor T. R. V. Murti, I also owe a debt of gratitude to Professor J. G. Arapura, who read and criticized parts of the manuscript, and to Professor Klaus Klostermaier, whose enthusiasm for and interest in Sphoṭa Theory has helped me to complete this book.

April, 1980 H. G. C.

CONTENTS

ABBREVIATIONS

Bṛhadāraṇyaka Upaniṣad	Br Up.
Chāndogya Upaniṣad	Ch. Up.
Kaṭha Upaniṣad	Ka. Up.
Maitri Upaniṣad	Mai. Up.
Māṇḍūkya Upaniṣad	Māṇḍ. Up.
Muṇḍaka Upaniṣad	Muṇḍ. Up.
Ṛgveda	R. V.
Śaṅkara's Bhāṣya or Brahmasūtra	Ś. B. B. S.
Sarva-Darśana-Saṁgraha	S. D. S.
Sphoṭasiddhi	Sph.
Taittirīya Brāhmaṇa	Tait. Br.
Taittirīya Upaniṣad	Tait. Up.
Vākyapadīya	Vāk.
Yoga Sūtras	Y. S.

CHAPTER ONE

LANGUAGE, ITS NATURE AND FUNCTION

In the beginning was the Word, and the Word was with God, and the Word was God.[1]

... *John*

Many who look do not see language, many who listen do not hear it. It reveals itself like a living and well adorned wife to her husband.[2]

... *Ṛgveda*

Aristotle established the classical Western conception of man as the being who has language (*logos*). Although animals can use signs and sounds to signal one another it would seem that man alone possesses the ability to think and to speak, and at the same time to be aware of what he is thinking and speaking. Language not only distinguishes man from the animals, it also mediates human knowledge. All knowledge of ourselves and all knowledge of the world comes to us through language.[3]

In spite of Aristotle's early observation of the importance of language, it is only recently that Western scholarship has begun seriously to study language. The extreme difficulty of this enterprise is at once evident. All thinking about language must, by virtue of human limitations, be done in language itself. One cannot get outside of language so as to objectively examine it. Language must be used to study language from within. In recognition of this difficulty a special name has been coined by scholars currently attempting this task. "Metalanguage" has been proposed to refer to language that theorizes about the nature of language.[4]

---

1. "The Gospel According to John" 1:1 *The Oxford Annotated Bible*.

2. Frits Staal, "Ṛgveda 10.71 on the origin of language", in Harold Coward and Krishna Sivaraman, eds., *Revelation in Indian Thought*, p. 5. Hereafter cited Staal, "Ṛgveda on 10.71".

3. Hans-Georg Gadamer, "Man and Language : in *Philosophical Hermeneutics*, trans. D. E. Linge, pp. 59-68. Hereafter cited Gadamer, *Man and Language*.

4. See, for example, Frits Staal, "The Concept of Metalanguage and Its Indian Background", in *Journal of Indian Philosophy*, III, (1975), pp. 315-354. Hereafter cited Staal, "The Concept of Metalanguage".

J. G. Herder and Wilhelm von Humboldt may be taken as the founders of modern Western linguistic science.[1] Emphasizing the naturalness of language, Herder and Humboldt developed an idealistic philosophy of language. Critical contributions to the study of language were also made by Kant and Hegel; Hegel called language the medium through which the subjective spirit is mediated with the being of objects.[2] In this century Ernest Cassirer has expanded the philosophy of language to include the natural sciences, the humanities, and all human cultural activity. He also recognizes that an essential characteristic of language is that it finds within itself its own criteria for truth and meaning. However, while the inclusiveness of Cassirer's perspective is to be applauded, there is one major point on which it is too narrow. Cassirer begins from the presupposition that language, art, and religion, are parallel "forms" of representation.[3] The difficulty here arises because of the fact that as far as human knowledge is concerned, all of it is encompassed within language. Art and religion are not "forms" separate from language but occur within language. Cassirer seems to be thinking of language in a too narrow and restricted sense.

A similar difficulty arises within a contemporary school of linguistic philosophy where language seems to be restricted to the printed word and then analyzed for a one to one correspondence with objective reality. All of this has the effect of reducing language to the formal or uttered word—something far removed from the idealistic notion of natural language from which Herder and von Humboldt, taking their cue from Aristotle, had started. As Klaus Klostermaier has observed, the approach of linguistic philosophy sees the word only as a 'carrier of information' and basically studies those aspects of language that a computer can store and retrieve...(However) the spoken word contains many dimensions that are inaccessible to the computer : dimensions we perceive when we labour to produce the right words for a thought; when we find ourselves struck by the appropriateness of a great poet's language; or when we rejoice in coining a word

1. Gadamer, *Man and Language*, p. 61.
2. Gadamer, "The Nature of Things" in *Philosophical Hermeneutics*, p. 76.
3. Ernst Cassirer, *Language and Myth*, pp. 8-9.

that seems to express uniquely what we feel."[1] While the computer-like function of language is highly respected, modern linguists seem to consign all other dimensions of the word to the unreality of a mystic's silence.[2] In their opinion, either the word is factual and scientific in its referent, or it is mystical and has no real function in life. When language is bifurcated into such extremes modern man is deprived of its fullness—and the fullness of reality which language in all its dimensions can manifest.

The Study of Language in Indian Thought

In contrast to the relatively recent stress on linguistics and the philosophy of language in the West, linguistic speculations were begun by the Hindus before the advent of recorded history.[3] Beginning with the Vedic hymns, which are at least 3,000 years old, the Indian study of language has continued in an unbroken tradition right upto the present day. The Indian approach to language was never narrow or restrictive. Language was examined in relation to consciousness—consciousness not constricted even to human consciousness. All aspects of the world and human experience were thought of as illuminated by language.

Indian philosophy postulated that language had both phenomenal and metaphysical dimensions. It is remarkable that in the ancient hymns of the *Ṛgveda* a semi-technical vocabulary was already developed to deal with such linguistic matters as language composition, poetic creation, inspiration, illumination, vision and so on.[4] Though there was careful concern for the phenomenal or outer aspects of language, the Indians always paid equal attention to the inner or metaphysical aspects of language. The Indians seem to have successfully avoided the two reductionistic mistakes of some schools of modern western

---

1. Klaus K. Klostermaier, "Man Carries the Power of All Things in His Mouth", in Coward and Sivaraman, in *Revelation in Indian Thought*, p. 88.

2. See, for example, Russell Fraser, *The Language of Adam*; see especially Chapter 4, "Mysticism and the Scientific Doom".

3. P. K. Chakravarti, *The Linguistic Speculations of the Hindus.*

4. Frits Staal, "The Concept of Metalanguage", p. 319.

language speculation. They did not reduce language to being a merely human convention having only scientific or factual referents; nor did they fall into the error of metaphysical reductionism which so devalues the meanings of human words that language ends up as obscure mysticism.[1] Grammarians like Pāṇini and Patañjali, and etymologists like Yāska were clearly concerned with human speech in the everyday empirical world; but they also made room for metaphysical study. Similarly, the great Indian philosopher of language, Bhartṛhari, begins his *Vākyapadiya* with a metaphysical enquiry into the nature and origin of language in relation to *Brahman*, but then goes on in Chapters Two and Three to explore technical grammatical points involved in the everyday use of language.[2] In classical Indian thought on language, the study of a given phenomenon and the contemplation of it as a metaphysical mystery do not preclude each other.

The ability of language to deal with ordinary human things and yet at the same time to be metaphysically grounded is further evidenced in the distinctive Indian notion of creativity. Here again the Indian approach shows itself to be more encompassing and insightful than the bifurcated and too narrow view of many of the modern western schools. Whereas modern man thinks of creativity in terms of a writer creating something "original" or "new", the classical Indian conception is quite different. As Klaus Klostermaier points out:

> The great creative geniuses of India, men like Gotama the Buddha or Śaṅkara, take care to explain their thought not as *creation* but as a retracing of forgotten eternal truth. They compare their activity to the clearing an overgrown ancient path in the jungle, not to the making of a new path.[3]

---

1. J. G. Arapura "Some Perspectives on Indian Philosophy of Language" in Coward and Sivaraman, *Revelation in Indian Thought*, p. 20. Hereafter cited Arapura, "Some Perspectives".

2. Bhartṛhari, *Vākyapadīya*, trans. K. A. S. Iyer.

3. Klaus Klostermaier, "The Creative Function of the Word" in "*Language*" *In Indian Philosophy and Religion*, ed. Harold Coward, p. 6. Klostermaier suggests that the scientific notion of "mirror-symmetries" may provide a helpful modern model for understanding the creative function of the word (as conceived in the classical traditions).

The creative effort of the *ṛṣi*—the composer or "seer" of the word—is not to manufacture something new out of his own imagination, but rather to relate ordinary things to their forgotten eternal truth. In this Indian perspective both the technical study of grammar and the philosophical analysis of language are seen as intellectual "brush-clearing" activities which together open the way for a rediscovery of the eternal truth in relation to everyday objects and events.

Language in the Vedas

Language (*vāk*) has a prominent place in the *Vedas*. *Vāk* is described as the support of gods such as Mitra-Varuṇa, Indra, Agni and the *Aśvins*. *Vāk* bends Rudra's bows against the sceptic and gathers up all prayers. In the *Śatapatha Brāhmaṇa* *vāk* is identified with Sarasvatī who later becomes known as the goddess of learning, wisdom and inspiration.[1] The action of the sages or *ṛṣis* in relation to language is highlighted in Frits Staal's translation of *Ṛgveda* 10.71 :[2]

> Bṛhaspati ! When they came forth to establish the first beginning of language, setting up names, what has been hidden in them as their best and purest good became manifest through love. (1)
>
> Where the sages fashioned language with their thought, filtering it like parched grain through a sieve, friends recognized their friendship. Their beauty is marked on the language. (2)
>
> They traced the course of language through ritual; they found it embodied in the seers. They gained access to it and distributed it widely; the seven chanters cheered them. (3) Many who look do not see language, many who listen do not hear it. It reveals itself like a loving and well adorned wife to her husband. (4)
>
> Though all the friends have eyes and ears, their mental intuitions are uneven. Some are like shallow ponds, which reach up to the mouth or armpit, others are like ponds which are fit for bathing. (7).

Here the power of language is clearly contrasted in its two forms. To those who "see", language (and meaning) is manifest, is

1. See *Ṛgveda* 10.125 and J. G. Arapura, "Some Perspectives", p. 21.
2. Frits Staal, "*Ṛgveda* 10.71", pp. 5-6.

widely distributed by the *ṛṣis*, is seen and heard with understanding, is self-revealing and provides for deep intuitions. By contrast, to those who do not "see", who are obstructed by their own ignorance, language (and meaning) is hidden, is mysteriously possessed by the *ṛṣis*, is looked at and listened to (without understanding), is wrongly used and is hidden from shallow intuitions.[1] According to this hymn, the nature and function of language is to manifest or reveal the meaning of things.

In the Vedas language is also directly identified with the Divine (*Brahman*). The *Ṛgveda* states that there are as many words as there are manifestations of *Brahman*.[2] Even in the later Hindu scriptures, the *Āraṇyakas* and *Upaniṣads*, there is a continued equating of speech and *Brahman*. As the *Bṛhadāraṇyaka Upaniṣad* states : *Vāg vai brahmeti*, "Speech, truly, is *Brahman*."[3]

In this respect there seem to be close parallels between the Brahmanical view that the *Veda* and *Brahman* are one, and the viewpoint expressed in Christian Scripture at the beginning of the Gospel according to Saint John, "In the beginning was the Word, and the Word was with God, and the Word was God." Both the Christian and the Brahmanical viewpoints seem to agree that speech and the Divine coexist. But there are significant differences that must be carefully noted. Whereas the Christian Scripture conceives of an absolute beginning of order when God speaks and through his speaking creates,[4] the Brāhmanical view believed in a cyclic view of creation with no absolute beginning. There may be beginning points for each cycle of creation, but there is no first cycle. The whole of the cosmos, in the Brahmanical view, has constantly been going on through cycles of creation-dissolution, creation-dissolution. . .beginninglessly. At the dissolution of each cycle a seed or trace (*saṁskāra*) is left behind out of which the next cycle arises. It is an agricultural image of seed-flower-seed. . . .

The significant thing to note in relation to the *Vedas* is that the nature of the seed, from which each cycle of creation bursts forth, is described as "Divine Word." Various symbols are used to indicate the divine nature of speech and its evolution to

1. Frits Staal, "*Ṛgveda* 10.71", pp. 8-9.
2. *Ibid.*, 5.10.2 and 10.114.8.
3. See *Bṛ. Up.* 4.1.2.
4. *John* 1:1 and *Genesis* 1.

form each cycle of creation. Professor Murti puts it well when he says, "The Brahmanical tradition stemming from the *Veda* takes language as of divine origin (*Daivī Vāk*), as Spirit descending and embodying itself in phenomena, assuming various guises and disclosing its real nature to the sensitive soul."[1] The "sensitive soul," in Brahmanical religion, was the seer, or *ṛṣi*—who has purged himself of ignorance, rendering his consciousness transparent to the Divine Word. The *ṛṣi* was not the individual composer of the Vedic hymn, but rather the seer (*draṣṭṛ*) of an eternal impersonal truth. As Aurobindo puts it, the language of the Veda is "rhythm not composed by the intellect but heard, a divine Word that came vibrating out of the Infinite to the inner audience of the man who had previously made himself fit for the impersonal knowledge."[2] The *ṛṣi*'s initial vision is said to be of the *Veda* as one, as a whole, the entirety of *Brahman*. This is represented in the *Māṇḍūkya Upaniṣad* by the mantra AUM, which includes within itself the three levels of ordinary consciousness—waking, dreaming, and deep sleep—yet also reaches out beyond to the transcendent where the sound itself comes to an end.[3] *Brahman* which is said to be beyond, is also said to be AUM.[4]

Language and the Prātiśākhyas

While the *Vedas* contained in seed form the essence of later Indian thought on language, it fell to the *Prātiśākhyas* to prescribe rules for prosody, phonetics, accentuation and *sandhi*[5] and thereby ensure that the oral form of the *Veda* would be preserved and passed on with little loss or distortion.[6] In the Indian tradition, language is thought to be truly and most fully

---

1. T. R. V. Murti, "Some Thoughts on the Indian Philosophy of Language". Presidential Address to the 37th Indian Philosophical Congress, 1963). p. viii. Hereafter cited Murti, "'Some Thoughts".

2. Aurobindo Ghose, *On the Veda*, p. 6. Hereafter cited Aurobindo, *Veda*.

3. J. G. Arapura, "Language and Phenomena", *Canadian Journal of Theology*. XVI, 1 and 2 (1970), p. 44.

4. See *Tait. Up*. 1.8.1.

5. *Sandhi* is a technical term in Sanskrit grammar which refers to the rules of euphonic combination.

6. Satyakam Varma, "Importance of the Prātiśākhyas" in *Studies In Indology*, pp. 32-52.

experienced only in its oral form. The written word is a secondary thing developed only for heuristic teaching purposes and as an aid for those too dull to remember the important texts by heart. For the Indian the criterion form of language is not written but oral, and the *Prātiśākhyas* play the important role of keeping the oral form disciplined and pure in its presentation. Knowledge of the *Vedas*, therefore, is not simply "book-learning" of the contents or main ideas, as is promoted by modern western scholarship. In the Indian tradition, language is considered to be fully alive only when spoken. Thus knowledge of the *Vedas* includes and requires the ability to speak the text with correct accent, metre and so on. The fact that the vast majority of the Vedic hymns are poems made attention to the details of form specified in the *Prātiśākhyas* even more important.

Stress on the oral or spoken form is an important aspect of the Indian view of language. Thinking is seen as internal speaking to which not enough *prāṇa* or breath energy has been added to make it overt. Writing is merely a coded recording which can never perfectly represent all the nuances of the spoken word, and is therefore always secondary. With regard to the relationship between written and spoken language, the Indian approach is opposite to that taken in modern western scholarship. In modern Biblical studies, for example, the aim of the scholar is to get back to the earliest available written manuscript and then to use that as a criterion against which to check the text that is in use today. Of paramount importance to this approach is the belief that, due to human failings, errors, such as mistakes in copying may have crept in over the years, which it is held, would not be present in the earlier manuscript. In addition the modern school of Form Criticism has argued that before many of the scriptures (e.g., the Gospel) were written down there was a period of oral transmission during which time the text (e.g., the original teachings of Jesus) was modified by the needs of the people and the particular conditions under which they lived. Thus the period of oral transmission is judged to have been unreliable due to its inability to carry forward the original sayings in a pure and unchanged form.[1]

1. See, for example, the fine critical survey of modern Biblical scholarship presented by Harvey McArthur in his "Introduction" to *In Search of the Historical Jesus*. The survey of Form Criticism is found on pp. 6-7.

The Indian practice is the exact opposite of this. When India achieved independence in 1947 one of the first acts of the new government was to establish a commission of senior scholars to go from place to place and listen to the assembled *Brahmins* reciting the *Vedas*. They would listen for errors in metre, accent, *sandhi* and for any loss or change in words. It was the rigorous practice of the *Prātiśākhyas* that was being checked by the senior scholars. They had mastered the *Prātiśākhyas* and pure presentation of the *Vedas* through many years of careful oral practice and checking with their teachers. The teachers of the present senior scholars had received it, not from books, but from oral practice with the best teachers of the generation before them, and so on in an unbroken oral tradition back to the *Vedas*. It is not the dead or entombed manuscript but the correct and clear speaking of the word in the here and now that makes for a living language and scripture. Large numbers of copies of "The Living Bible" stacked in bookstores or reverently placed on personal bookshelves are not true language or living scripture according to the Indian. Only when a passage is so well learned that it is with one wherever one goes, is the word really known. In such a state the words become part of, or even more exactly *are* one's consciousness in the act of speaking. Books and all written forms are not knowledge in this sense of the word, and represent, for the Indian, a lower, inferior, second order of language suitable only for the dull or the uneducated. The *Prātiśākhyas* are the training rules for the oral learning of language and the preservation of the vedic word in its pure form.

Indian Grammarians and Philosophers of Language

From the *Vedas* upto the present, the study of grammar and the philosophy of language has occupied a central place in Indian thought. In the earliest *Prātiśākhyas*, or rules for speaking the *Vedas*, the first formulations of Sanskrit Grammar may be found. Before the time of Buddha (i.e. before 600 B.C.) the *Prātiśākhyas* alongside the *Brāhmaṇas*, *Upaniṣads* and *Niruktas* (etymologies) were being developed. From this early period upto 1000 A.D. Sanskrit dominated and rapidly became the national language of India.[1] As Sanskrit became standardized

1. Satyakam Varma, "Sanskrit : A Living Tradition" in *Studies In Indology*, p. 59.

a regular grammar developed. This grammar was not an artificial construct of the scholars but rather developed directly and naturally from the spoken language. Space does not allow a detailed recounting of this development. Concise surveys are available in the literature.[1]

The oldest etymology available is the *Nirukta* of Yāska. Pāṇini, the widely known Sanskrit grammarian, mentions a number of other grammarians who preceded him. Patañjali[2] wrote the important commentary on Pāṇini's *sūtras*, and many others have written glosses on Patañjali. In addition there have been rearrangements of the Pāṇini *sūtras* with other lines of interpretation arising (e.g. *Siddhānta-kaumudi* of Bhaṭṭoji-Dīkṣita).[3] The overall aim of the Sanskrit grammarians was not to artificially standardize language, but to bring out the intended meaning. As Yāska put it, it is to get to the real meaning of an uttered work (*arthanityaḥ parikṣeta*).[4] Sanskrit grammar was an attempt to discipline and explain the behaviour of a spoken language, so that the inner meaning could shine forth unobstructed.

It was this latter aspect, the perceiving of the intended meaning, that commanded the attention of the Indian philosophers of language. Among the many excellent Indian philosophers of language (e.g. Maṇḍana Miśra, Kumārila, Kauṇḍabhaṭṭa, Abhinavagupta, etc.) Bhartṛhari[5] (580 A.D.) consistently ranks as the most important. In Bhartṛhari's major work, the *Vākyapadiya*, the ways in which Indian philosophy conceives the outer word form to be united with its inner meaning are discussed. Bhartṛhari's own position has come to be known as the *Sphoṭa* Theory after the Sanskrit term *sphuṭ*, which means "to burst forth" or when applied to language "a bursting forth of illumination or insight." V. S. Apte in his *Sanskrit-English*

---

1. See, e.g., Satyakam Varma's "A Brief Survey of Sanskrit Grammar" in *Studies In Indology*, pp. 103-143.

2. This Patañjali may or may not be the same Patañjali who is the author of the *Yoga-sūtras*. Dasgupta argues for their identity, J. H. Woods argues against it. See Surendranath Dasgupta, *A History of Indian Philosophy*, I, pp. 231-238 for a concise summary of both arguments.

3. H. T. Cole Brooke, "On the Sanskrit and Prakrit Languages" in *A Reader on the Sanskrit Grammarians*, ed. J. F. Staal, pp. 35-45.

4. See *Nirukta*, 2.1.1.

5. For a beginner's introduction see Harold G. Coward, *Bhartṛhari*.

Dictionary defines *sphoṭa* as the idea that bursts out or flashes on the mind when a sound is uttered.[1]

Bhartṛhari's Sphoṭa Theory of Language

The original conception of *sphoṭa* seems to come from early in the Vedic period of Indian thought. *Vāk* or speech was taken as a manifestation of the all-pervading *Brahman*. The *mantra* AUM was regarded as the primordial speech-sound from which all forms of *vāk* are thought to have evolved. This sacred syllable is said to have flashed forth into the heart of *Brahman* while he was absorbed in deep meditation, and to have given birth to the *Vedas* containing all knowledge. At the very beginning of the *Vākyapadiya*, Bhartṛhari restates these very teachings as the foundation for his own thinking.[2] Just as the original unitary *Veda* has been handed down in many ways by the *ṛṣis* for the sake of communication, so also the unitary *sphoṭa* is manifested as a series of uttered sounds for the purposes of expression and communication. Although the various manifestations of the one Veda may vary in form and style of expression (*dhvani*) from poet to poet and from region to region, it is the same truth (*dharma*) that is being expressed throughout.

Although Bhartṛhari may have based his theory of language on the vedic AUM, his method of approach was strikingly different. Rather than just immersing himself in the mystical chanting of AUM, he sets out to analyze the meanings of words and the means by which such word knowledge is manifested and communicated in ordinary experience. Bhartṛhari develops his theory of language by maintaining that the *sphoṭa*, the meaning-whole, is something over and above the uttered or written letters.[3] The individual letter sounds (*dhvani*) vary with the speaker (accent, speed of delivery, etc.) but this does not matter since they are uttered only for the purpose of manifesting the changeless *sphoṭa* which exists within the speaker and is potentially present within the consciousness of every hearer. The *dhvanis*, the apparent external differences, are simply various

1. V. S. Apte, *The Practical Sanskrit-English Dictionary*, p. 1013.

2. *Vākyapadīya of Bhartṛhari*, ed. K. A. Subramania Iyer, 1:5-10. All quotations from the *Vākyapadīya* are taken from this translation.

3. John Brough, "Theories of General Linguistics in the Sanskrit Grammarians" in *A Reader on the Sanskrit Grammarians*, ed. J. F. Staal, p. 411.

external manifestations of the one internal *sphoṭa*. The process of ordinary communication is explained as follows. At first the word exists in the mind of the speaker as a unity or *sphoṭa*. When he utters it, he produces a sequence of different sounds so that it appears to have differentiation. The listener, although first hearing a series of sounds, ultimately perceives the utterance as a unity—"the light bulb coming on" image of the cartoon. This "ah ha !" experience of the listener is his mental perception of the same *sphoṭa* with which the speaker began, and it is then that the meaning of the word first seen by the speaker is also known by the hearer. Contrary to most theories of communication, Bhartṛhari's view is that meaning is not conveyed from the speaker to the hearer, rather, the spoken words serve only as the stimulus to reveal or uncover the meaning which was already present in the mind of the hearer.[1]

Returning to the experience of the poet, the central or essential idea of the poem is a given that is inherently present in the poet's consciousness—and in the consciousness of everyone else. At the first moment of its revelation the poet is completely caught up into this unitary idea or *sphoṭa*. But when he starts to examine the idea with an eye to its communication he has withdrawn himself from the first intimate unity with the idea or inspiration itself, and now experiences it in a twofold fashion. On the one hand there is the objective meaning (*artha*), which he is seeking to communicate, and on the other are the words and phrases (*dhvanis*) he will utter. For Bhartṛhari these two aspects of word-sound (*dhvani*) and the word-meaning (*artha*), differentiated in the mind and yet integrated like two sides of the same coin, constitute the *sphoṭa*. Bhartṛhari emphasizes the meaning-bearing or revelatory function of this two-sided unity, the *sphoṭa*, which he maintains is eternal[2] and inherent in consciousness.[3]

When a child is learning a word or an adult is trying to grasp an idea, the first cognition is often erroneous. Having failed to grasp the whole *sphoṭa*, the listener asks, "What did you say ?" As the speaker repeats the same words, or perhaps uses

1. John Brough, "Theories of General Linguistics in the Sanskrit Grammarians" in *A Reader on the Sanskrit Grammarians*. ed. J. F. Staal, 1:44-46.

2. *Ibid.*, 1:23-26.

3. *Ibid.*, 1:122-123.

different words in attempting to communicate the same idea, there arises a progressively clearer cognition of the *sphoṭa*. Finally there is a completely clear cognition of the whole *sphoṭa* and its two-sided aspect. This Bhartṛhari describes as a case of special perception or intuition (*pratibhā*).[1] In a more philosophic sense, *sphoṭa* may be described as the transcendent ground in which the spoken syllables and the conveyed meanings find themselves united.

Maṇḍana Miśra illustrates Bhartṛhari's theory with the analogy of a jeweller who assesses the genuineness of a precious stone. His continuous gaze is really a series of cognitions, each of which perceives the genuineness of the stone but with increasing clarity. Each cognition leaves its *saṁskāra* or common memory trace. The last cognition, helped by the *saṁskāra* of the previous one, fully perceives the genuineness of the stone; but for the *saṁskāras* of the intervening cognitions, there would be no difference between the last one and the first one. An important point is that the jeweller is described as "expert", meaning that before beginning the examination he already had the image of a precious stone ingrained in his subconscious, and it was this image (like the inhering *sphoṭa*) which was revealed to the jeweller's mind by his series of partial (and since partial, also erroneous) perceptions.[2]

Maṇḍana also offers the example of a picture. He points out that in our cognition of a picture, although we may be aware of the different parts and colours, the picture is perceived as a whole which is over and above its parts. Similarly, when we perceive a piece of cloth our cognition is of the cloth as a whole and is quite distinct from the various threads and colours involved.[3]

In these examples there is a necessary perception of the parts prior to the perception of the whole. This aspect is brought out clearly by Bhartṛhari who describes the painter as going through three stages when he paints a picture : "When a painter

---

1. John Brough, "Theories of General Linguistics in the Sanskrit Grammarians" in *A Reader on the Sanskrit Grammarians*, ed. J. F. Staal, I:83-84.

2. *The Sphoṭasiddhi of Maṇḍana Miśra* trans. K. A. Subramania Iyer, *kārikā* 18 ff, pp. 43 ff. All quotations from *Sph.* are taken from this translation.

3. *Ibid.*, *kārikā* 24, p. 64.

wishes to paint a figure having parts like that of a man, he first sees it gradually in a sequence, then as the object of a single cognition, and then paints it on cloth or on a wall in sequence."[1] So also the hearer of a word perceives the word in a sequence of letters which manifest in him the whole word as the object of a single cognition. As a speaker, however, he utters the whole word in its differentiated appearance as a sequence of letters. It is in this context that the perception of the many letters, before the final perception of the unitary *sphoṭa*, is described as error, illusion, or appearance. But it is a unique kind of error in that it has a fixed sequence and form, it ultimately leads to the perception of the truth, and is thus regarded as a universal error.[2] The chief cause of this universal error is described as *avidyā* or the limitation of the individual self-consciousness. A characteristic of this *avidyā* is that it provides no other means for cognizing the *sphoṭa*, except the letters. That is why all individual selves universally experience the same error with regard to speech, but it is an error which ultimately leads to cognition of truth. It is only through this error or appearance of differentiation that the individual *sphoṭa* comes within the range of worldly usage so that we ordinary mortals have a way of comprehending it.[3]

From what has been said thus far it is clear that in Bhartṛhari's philosophy language may be seen to operate on at least two levels. On one level there is *pratibhā* or the intuitive flashlike understanding of the meaning of the sentence, book or poem as a whole. On the other level there are the uttered sounds which go together to make up the sentence, book or poem. Bhartṛhari calls the latter *vaikhari vāk* or outer speech, while the former is aptly designated as *paśyanti vāk* or inner speech that directly sees or perceives reality.[4] Between these two levels, says

1. *Vāk.*, I:52.

2. If one moves beyond Sanskrit itself and into the world of languages, I would take the "universal error" to refer to the necessity of going from the differentiated letters ("error") to the whole *sphoṭa* (meaning or ultimate reality). The fixed sequence and form of differentiation for a particular word-*sphoṭa* would only be a constant error within each language (such as Sanskrit).

3. *Vāk.*, I:85.

4. *Ibid.*, I:142.

Bhartṛhari, there is a middle or *madhyamā vāk*. This middle level is the level of thought. Here the unitary *sphoṭa* appears separated into its sequence of thoughts, words and phrases none of which have as yet reached the level of uttered sound. According to Bhartṛhari these are the three levels through which *vāk* or language passes whenever one speaks. *Vāk*, which is at first quite internal, is gradually externalized for the purpose of speaking. Hearing of course operates in the reverse direction. In this way Bhartṛhari accounts for the complete continuum of cognition. Whether one is dealing with factual scientific language or a poem which can be understood on various levels, Bhartṛhari's *Sphoṭa* Theory would seem to provide an adequate explanation.

The logic of Bhartṛhari's philosophy of language is that the whole is prior to the parts. This results in an ascending hierarchy of speech levels. The word is subsumed by the sentence, the sentence by the paragraph, the paragraph by the chapter, the chapter by the book, and so on, until all speech is identified with *Brahman*.

In spite of the importance of language as the distinguishing feature of human consciousness and the medium through which all human knowledge passes, the study of linguistics and the philosophy of language in the west has only been seriously pursued in recent times. Today's modern scientific study suffers from focusing on the outer words especially in written form. Even a cursory look at the long and fully developed Indian study of language strongly suggests that the nature of the language may be more complex and powerful than modern thought would lead us to suspect.

The benefits of an oral based tradition of language seem significant enough to lead us to further examine the sophisticated development of language in Indian thought. A study of *Sphoṭa* Theory, as formulated by Bhartṛhari seems especially promising. It is to this task that the remainder of the book is devoted.

PART I

METAPHYSICAL BACKGROUND OF THE SPHOṬA THEORY

In Part One, a conceptual survey of Indian thought regarding language and revelation is undertaken. The purpose of this survey is to make clear the metaphysical background against and out of which the *Sphoṭa* Theory of language as revelation develops.

The Indian literature on the nature of language is vast. Each of the different philosophic *darśanas* ("viewpoints") have put forth their own view of language and its revelatory power, and criticized the views of others. Consequently, a comprehensive review of the whole debate cannot possibly be undertaken. Such a study would be a work of enormous compass.

Yet, for the Western reader especially, some background knowledge is a necessary prerequisite for an adequate understanding of the *Sphoṭa* theory. To draw out such a brief conceptual survey from the voluminous Indian debate over language has necessitated the adoption of some method of selection. Here I have adopted the approach of Professor T. R. V. Murti.[1] He suggests that in the Indian debate regarding the nature of language two principal traditions may be identified: the Brahmanical tradition stemming from the scriptures, which holds that language is divine in origin; and the Naturalistic tradition of the *Cārvāka* and earlier Buddhism, which holds that language is an arbitrary and conventional tool. This categorizing of the various schools of Indian thought into two traditions is not done without difficulty. For example, there are often strong and definite differences between two schools categorized within the same tradition, and sometimes even within a single school major quarrels erupt. Then again, certain *darśanas* such as the *Jaina* and *Nyāya* seem to occupy an intermediary position between the two traditions. Yet in spite of these difficulties, the purpose of achieving a brief but representative overview seems best pursued by examining selected schools from each of these two traditions.

1. See T. R. V. Murti, "Some Thoughts".

Chapter Two begins with an outline of the Brahmanical tradition as it is evidenced in the Hindu scriptures, as well as in the *Mīmāṁsā*, the *Sāṅkhya-Yoga* and the *Vedānta* schools of Indian philosophy. In Chapter Three, the Naturalistic tradition of the *Cārvāka* and early Buddhism is examined, along with the *Jaina* and *Nyāya* as occupying a somewhat intermediary position. The development of the *Sphoṭa* approach is traced against the "two traditions" background in Chapter Four.

CHAPTER TWO

LANGUAGE IN THE BRAHMANICAL TRADITION[1]

Indian speculations on the nature of language began very early.[2] In the *Ṛgveda* several hymns are devoted to *Vāk* (Speech) and the same trends are continued in the *Brāhmaṇas* and the *Upaniṣads*.[3] Speech is described as the creation of the gods.[4] It permeates all of creation.[5] The Brahmanical tradition goes further yet in identifying language with the divine. The *Ṛgveda* states that there are as many words as there are manifestations of Brahman.[6] The *Āraṇyakas* and early *Upaniṣads* continue to equate Speech and *Brahmon*; as one of the early *Āraṇyakas* states, the whole of Speech is *Brahman*.[7] In the *Taittiriya Brāhmaṇa*, Speech is seen as the support of all creation.[8] Various symbols are used to indicate the divine nature of Speech and its evolution to form creation. Prajāpati and Speech are viewed as male and female copulating to create the world.[9] Professor Murti puts it well when he says,

> The Brahmanical tradition stemming from the Veda takes language as of Divine origin (Daivī Vāk), as Spirit descending and embodying itself in phenomena, assuming various guises and disclosing its real nature to the sensitive soul. The well-known Ṛgveda verse, "Catvāri śṛṅgāḥ" expresses this truth

1. The term "tradition" here is not used in the sense of doctrine which is supposed to have divine authority, but to mean the source from which flows a continuous stream of thought and culture.

2. P. K. Chakravarti, *The Linguistic Speculations of the Hindus*, pp. 1-11. These early speculations included reflections on the origins of language, the relation of words with their meaning, the question of whether speech is eternal or created and considerations as to the nature of speech in its original state.

3. Murti, "Some Thoughts," p. vi.

4. RV. 10.10.125.3.

5. RV. 10.10.114.8.

6. RV. 5.10.2 and 10.114.8.

7. *Sāṅkhya Āraṇyako*, 3.3.

8. *Tait. Br*. 2.8.8.4-5.

9. *Tāṇḍya Mbr*. 20.14.2 and *Kaṭha Brāhmaṇa* 12.5.

in poetic form. It symbolizes speech as the Bellowing Bull of abundant fecundity, as the Great God descending into the sphere of the mortals (Mahādevo martyām āviveśa).[1]

In the *Upaniṣads* speculations on language become more philosophical. *Brahman* is defined as the one reality, without a second, and is identified with Speech.[2] But the question then arises as to how this single absolute real can be expressed by the many words when the former is defined as "one without a second". As Arapura has observed, the *Māṇḍūkya Upaniṣad* tries to link the unspeakable Absolute with the speakable through speech itself. "It creates the deeply meaningful symbol of AUM, which traversing the three phenomenal levels of consciousness, waking, dreaming and deep sleep, reaches out beyond to the transcendent where the sound itself comes to an end."[3] *Brahman,* which is said to be Speech is also said to be AUM.[4] Just as leaves are held together by a stalk, so is all speech held together by AUM.[5] In both the *Upaniṣads* and the *Ṛgveda,* speech is seen to have various levels ranging from the manifoldness of the phenomenal words to the absolute oneness of *Brahman* as *Vāk.*[6] The implication is that only as we perceive speech at its higher levels do we get a clear revelation of its meaning. Thus it is said that the ignorant man seeing and hearing speech in its overt manifest forms does not know its real nature. "To the wise, Speech reveals her intrinsic nature, even as the loving wife does to her lord. Lost in appearances we fail to penetrate to the deeper reality."[7] The *Sāṅkhya-Yoga, Mīmāṁsā, Vedānta,* the school of Grammar and Kashmir Śaivism are not only loyal to this tradition but give further systematic development to these early "seed" concepts. But before looking at some of these schools, let us briefly examine the approaches of the vedic and upaniṣadic seers (*ṛṣis*) to the divine *Vāk.*

---

1. Murti, "Some Thoughts", p. viii.
2. Br. Up. 4.1.2.
3. J. G. Arapura, "Language and Phenomena", in *Canadian Journal of Theology,* xvi, 1 and 2 (1970), p. 44.
4. See Tai. Up. 1.8.1.
5. See Ch. Up. 2.23.3.
6. RV. 2.3.22 and 10.2 Māṇḍ. Up.
7. See Murti, "Some Thoughts".

The Approaches of the Ṛṣi to the Divine Vāk

The Vedic seers are called in Sanskrit, *Ṛṣis*, defined by Monier-Williams as, "a singer of sacred hymns, an inspired poet or sage, any person who alone or with others invokes the deities in rhythmical speech or song of a sacred character, e.g. Kutsa, Atri, Rebha, Agastya, etc."[1] The root given is *ṛṣ* which, it is suggested, is perhaps from an obsolete root *ṛṣ* for root *dṛś*, "to see." Consequently, the *Ṛṣis* are said to be the "seers" rather than the authors of the Vedic hymns. The approach of the Vedic *Ṛṣis* to the real characterized not by logical reasoning but rather by intuitive inspiration or illumination. He was not the individual composer of the hymn, but rather the seer *draṣṭṛ* of an eternal impersonal truth. As Aurobindo describes it,

> The language of Veda itself is *śruti*, a rhythm not composed by the intellect but heard, a divine Word that came vibrating out of the Infinite to the inner audience of the man who had previously made himself fit for the impersonal knowledge. The words themselves, *dṛṣṭi* and *śruti*, sight and hearing, are Vedic expressions; these and cognate words signify, in the esoteric terminology of the hymns, revelatory knowledge and the contents of inspiration.[2]

Aurobindo emphasizes that the approach of the *Ṛṣi* is not aimed at speculation or aesthetic originality but rather the practical achievement of the spiritual goal—the divine vision—by himself and for others around him.

Another author has made a careful philological study of this vision of the Vedic *Ṛṣis*. Such a vision, says J. Gonda, comes to the mind in a spontaneous flash of intuition (*dhi*) which is beyond all purely sensuous perception.[3] In his approach to the real the Vedic *Ṛṣi* is thought of as having been "emptied of himself" and "filled with the god." Therefore the words that he spoke were not his own words, but the words of the god. This suprahuman origin lent his words a healing, a salutary power, and made them even into a deed of salvation. It is this

1. M. Monier-Williams, *A Sanskrit-English Dictionary*, p. 226.
2. See Aurobindo, *Veda*, p. 6.
3. J. Gonda, *The Vision of the Vedic Poets*, p. 17. Hereafter cited Gonda, *Vision*.

understanding of the true word as being at once inherently powerful and inherently teleological that is so difficult for modern Western minds to comprehend. Yet these are the very characteristics that underlie Indian cultic ritual and chant. From this viewpoint duly formulated and rhythmically pronounced words are bearers of power. This, as Gonda makes clear, has given rise to the traditional Indian belief that formulas are a decisive power, that whoever utters a mantra sets power in motion. "It has conditioned belief in the suprahuman power of the verses and stanzas of the *Veda*, in the eternity and suprahuman nature of the *Veda* in its entirety."[1] The texts come to be judged as formal expressions of ultimate reality, revealed by *dhi* or "vision" and recited as a rite to actualize their inherent power and affect both the worshipper and the gods involved—to further the teleological process of the whole cosmos.[2]

A point of agreement between Aurobindo and Gonda is that this "inner or central meaning," with all its potential power and teleology, is not simply given to the *Ṛṣi* in its finished form. Aurobindo describes it as a living thing; a thing of power, creative, formative; a primitive root-word with an immense progeny; a general character or quality (*guṇa*) capable of many applications—thus he accounts for "the enormous number of different meanings of which a single word was capable and also the enormous number of words which could be used to represent a single idea."[3] This also is the key distinction for Vedic interpretation or translation for Aurobindo—to locate the root-word meaning, put it in place of the obscure word in the text, and then test for validity by checking the sense of the root-meaning in the overall context. Gonda makes a similar point by showing that an analysis of the Vedic term *dhiḥ* makes clear that the more revelation of a "vision" or "central meaning" was not enough. Having received such a supranormal "vision", the *Ṛṣi* still had the task of fostering and cultivating the *dhiḥ* which had come to him. "He had to translate it into audible and intelligible words . . . to develop the initial nucleus into a more or less coherent series of stanzas."[4] In this sense Gonda

1. Gonda, *Vision*, p. 64.
2. *Ibid.*
3. Aurobindo, *Veda*, p. 57.
4. Gonda, *Vision*, p. 106.

finds *dhiḥ* to be frequently identified by the vedic poets with a cow. Indra and Varuṇa are likened to two bulls of a cow, lovers of *dhiḥ*, fertilizing and generating divine *Vāk*. Just as a milch cow gives us refreshing food and drink, so also the hymn (cow) which originated in a vision, will swell with milk.[1] The symbolism here indicates that the gods also play a part in the realization of the religious vision. Agni's activity with regard to *dhiyaḥ* is described as "help" or "good offices;"[2] "help" probably both in receiving the proper visionary *Vāk*, and in making them into effective verses.

It seems clear from this discussion that the *Ṛṣi*, according to the ancient Indian tradition was not a speculative philosopher but rather an intuitive receiver of the divine revelation of *Vāk*. This revelation was a solitary vision carrying its own intrinsic power, validity and objective reality. The poetic form of the expression of the vision left it open to various levels of interpretation and apprehension by those who heard it from the *Ṛṣi*. On a lower level, many of the hymns might be taken to represent a naturalistic and polytheistic approach to reality. But, on a higher level, it can also be held that the visions of the Vedic *Ṛṣis* evidence a monotheistic approach in which the various Vedic gods are simply descriptive names representing the various manifestations of tne one Deity or Reality.[3] Aurobindo also finds that spiritual realization by identity, which is so central to the *Upaniṣads*, is present in the experience of the Vedic *Ṛṣi* :

> (The hymn) rose out of his soul, it became a power of his mind, it was the vehicle of his self-expression . . . . It helped him to express the god in him, to destroy the devourer, the expresser of evil.[4]

The continuity from the Vedic hymns to the *Brāhmaṇas* and finally to the *Upaniṣads* is evident in many ways. The intuitive vision (*dhi*) of the Vedic *Ṛṣi* is still very much present in the *Brāhmaṇas*. For example, in a series of *mantras*, Indra's *dhiyaḥ* are said to be yoked (*yuj-dhiyaḥ*) or made use of for self-

---

1. RV. 2.2.9.
2. RV. 1.79.7.
3. Aurobindo, *Veda*, p. 9.
4. *Ibid.*, p. 13.

realization.[1] On a lower level, the sacrificial ritual, which had been present to some degree in the Vedic hymns, was given greater development and importance in the *Brāhmaṇas*. This meant that the *Ṛṣi* of the Vedic hymns, the inspired singer of truth, now tends to become the possessor of a revealed scripture and the repeater of a magical formula.[2] But while the majority of *Brāhmins* during the period of the *Brāhmaṇas* may have concentrated on establishing an authoritative systematization (*Śabda-pramāṇa*) of the ritual sacrificial aspects of the Vedic hymns, there were always some inspired teachers who resisted rigid formalizing and focused on the subjective spirituality of the Vedic visions. Due to their efforts, evidence may be found in the *Brāhmaṇas* of early struggles towards the formulation of many of the philosophic statements of the Upaniṣadic Seers.[3]

In continuity with this spiritual group of Brahmanical thinkers, the *Ṛṣi* of the *Upaniṣads* sought to recover the ancient spirit and knowledge of the Vedic Seers by philosophic meditation and spiritual experience. As Aurobindo puts it :

> ...they (the Upaniṣadic Ṛṣis) used the text of the ancient mantras as a prop or an authority for their own intuitions and perceptions; or else the Vedic Word was a seed of thought and vision by which they recovered old truths in new forms. What they found, they expressed in other terms more intelligible to the age in which they lived. In a certain sense their handling of the texts was not disinterested.... They were seekers of a higher than verbal truth and used words merely as suggestions for the illumination towards which they were striving.[4]

This quotation from Aurobindo highlights several aspects of the approach of the Upaniṣadic Seers, which we will now examine.

First, they experienced and further clarified the vision of *Vāk* which had previously been seen by the Vedic *Ṛṣis*. Gonda gives evidence for this in his study which shows that the *dhī* or vision of the Vedic Seers is also central to the approach of the *Upaniṣads*.[5] In the *Upaniṣads* the adjective *dhīra* characterizes

1. Tait. Br., 2.5.3.2.
2. Radhakrishnan, *Indian Philosophy*, I, p. 125.
3. *Ibid.*, pp. 130-36.
4. Aurobindo, *Veda*, p. 16.
5. Gonda, *Vision*, See Ch. IX, pp. 245-358.

the one who clearly sees the true and fundamental nature of reality.[1] In keeping with their increasingly precise analysis, the Upaniṣadic Seers make clear that this supersensuous *dhi* is a function of the mind rather than the senses.[2] It is this psychic faculty (*dhi*) which enables the *Ṛṣi* to penetrate into the world of the unseen reality—even to the ultimate vision of his own true Self (*Ātman*).[3] The more exact expression of the nature of the Real as seen via the *dhi* is the unique contribution of the Upaniṣadic Seers. Whereas the *Saṁhitās* of the *Ṛgveda* give external, cosmic, poetic expression to this vision of the underlying unity of all reality,[4] the Upaniṣadic Seers adopt the approach of philosophic dialogue and "negative exclusion" to help the truth seeker attain inner vision of ultimate unity (*Ātman*=*Brahman*).

A second aspect of the Upaniṣadic approach is the characteristic focusing upon or reference to the Vedic word or mantra by the *Ṛṣi*. For example, in discussing the nature of the creation of this world the *Ṛṣi* of the *Bṛhadāraṇyaka Upaniṣad* refers back to envisioned words, "I was Manu and the sun"[5] by the Vedic Seer Vāmadeva as the basis and authority for his contention. "This is so now also. Whoever thus knows 'I am Brahma' becomes this All; even the gods have no power to prevent his becoming thus, for he becomes their self (*ātman*)."[6] By focusing on the Vedic intuition of the underlying unity between the *Ṛṣi*, the gods and the real, the Upaniṣadic Seer brings out clearly the Philosophic and religious implications of the vision, i.e., creation consists of *Brahman* becoming the All (including gods, seers, men, etc.), and whenever one awakens to this truth he immediately realizes that his essence or Self is identical with

1. Gonda, *Vision*, p. 253.
2. Br. Up. 1.5.3.
3. Mai. Up., 6.25.
4. See, e.g., RV. X.168, "The Ātman of the Gods, the germ of the world...;" III.54 "One all is lord of...this multiform creation"; X.121 "...the one life-spirit of the Gods...the one God above the Gods..." and references to *Ṛta*. Translations from Sarvepalli Radhakrishnan and Charles A. Moore, eds., *A Sourcebook in Indian Philosophy*, pp. 15, 22, 25.
5. R.V. 4.26.1.
6. Br. Up. 1.4.10, See Robert Ernest Hume, trans., *The Thirteen Principal Upanishads*, pp. 83-84.

Brahman. Therefore, to worship God as some divinity other than one's Self is ignorance.

A third aspect of the Upaniṣadic approach is also illustrated in the above example. Whereas in the Vedic hymns and the *Brāhmaṇas*, the vision is usually verbalized in external mythical symbols (such as Manu and the sun), the Upaniṣadic seers adopt increasingly abstract ("this All") and internal (*Ātman* or Self is *Brahman*) symbols in their verbalization of the Real.[1] This process of increasing philosophic abstraction and internalization reaches its peak, in one sense, with the "negative exclusion" teaching of "not this, not that" (*neti*, *neti*). By this *via negative* philosophic approach, the Upaniṣadic *Ṛṣis* force their students beyond all possible conceptualizations to the realization of a higher than speakable truth which is symbolized by the *turiya* level of *AUM* in the *Māṇḍūkya Upaniṣad*. As one *Ṛṣi* puts it, *neti*, *neti* leads us to the understanding that there is nothing higher than the realization that he is *not this*—but the underlying Reality ("the Real of the real") upon which all particularization as "this" or "that" depends.[2]

A fourth aspect of the Upaniṣadic approach relates to the context naturally fostered by the philosophic method outlined above. Whereas the Vedic Seer spoke his vision in the form of solitary hymn (evoking responses at the varying levels of ritual sacrifice, worshipful devotion or, for some, self-realization), the Upaniṣadic *Ṛṣi* spoke his vision within the context of the teacher-pupil relationship.[3] Consequently, the common form

---

1. It should be noted here that this Upaniṣadic approach was not completely unknown to the Vedic *Ṛṣis*. For example, a remarkable symbolization of the real in very abstract terms occurs in *RV*. 10.129 where the underlying principle of all (including all the gods) is *tad ekaṁ sat*, "that One Being." On the other hand, it is also true that the theistic approach to the real, which is dominant in the Vedic hymns, is also to be found in the *Upaniṣads*. As Dasgupta points out, a minor current of thought in the *Upaniṣads* is that of theism which looks upon *Brahman* as the Lord controlling the world. It is because of this unsystematized variety of approaches in the *Upaniṣads* that differing schools of philosophy (e.g., Śaṅkara and Rāmānuja) can appeal to the *Upaniṣads* for support.

2. Bṛ. Up. 2.3.6 and Māṇḍ. Up. 7.

3. The word *Upaniṣad* comes from the Sanskrit prefixes *upa* and *ni* plus the root *Sad*, which means "sitting down near" i.e. the teacher to receive instruction. See Muṇḍ. Up. I.2.12 and 13.

is one of philosophic probing towards the Real by question and answer. A good example of this approach occurs in Br. Up. 2.4.5, which relates a dialogue between the sage Yājñavalkya and his wife Maitreyī as he leads her towards the realization that "it is the *Ātman* that should be seen. . .and with the understanding of the *Ātman*, this world-all is known."[1] The goal of this teaching relationship is repeatedly described by the Upaniṣadic *Ṛṣis* as the student's intuitive vision of the identity between himself and the real (between *Ātman* and *Brahman*). This is the essence of the Four Great Teachings or *Mahāvākyas* : *tat tvam asi*, "that thou art;" *aham Brahma asmi*, "I am Brahman;" *ayam ātmā Brahma*, "This *Ātman* is *Brahman*;" and *prajñānam Brahma*, "Consciousness is *Brahman*." The purpose of the philosophic dialogue preceding the statement of the *Mahāvākya* by the *Ṛṣi* is to systematically remove the obstructions (*avidyā*) in the mind of the student, which are preventing him from directly perceiving the Real (*Brahman*). The systematic use of *anumāna* or reasoning in removing defects such as contrary notions so that the unshakable immediate experience of *Brahman* can arise is characteristic of the Upaniṣadic approach to the Real.[2] Various tactics are adopted by the *Ṛṣi* in their use of reasoning. One tactic is to seek to identify the essence of the empirical world with its subjective underlying unity.[3] In such approaches the common method is to start with the gross and then reason towards the subtle.[4] Another tactic used by the *Ṛṣi* is to approach the Real by questions which seek to lay bare the reality underlying all change and suffering,[5] but perhaps the most difficult aspect of all these methods is the wisdom required for the admission that one's own intellectual prowess and system-building achievements do not attain for him the Real.[6] The use of the intellect will help by removing the obstructions of wrong idea. In the end, however, all price, even in such meritorious achievement as knowledge of the *Veda* itself, must be overcome by spiritual and mental discipline

1. Bṛ. Up. 2.4.5 Hume, *Thirteen*, p. 100.
2. T. M. P. Mahadevan, *The Philosophy of Advaita*, p. 57.
3. Muṇḍ. Up. 1.1.3.
4. Bṛ. Up. 4.3.1-6.
5. Ch. Up. 6.2.1 ff. and 6.13-6.15; Ka. Up. 1.20 ff.
6. Ka. Up. 2.23; Bṛ. Up. 4.4.21 and 3.5.1.

(*Yoga*) so that the intuition of the Real can occur.[1] In this direct vision, the *Ṛṣi* finds the Real to be the overflowing of peace and bliss or *ānanda* upon which all life depends.[2]

This brief survey has shown that for the *Ṛṣis* of the *Saṁhitā*, the *Brāhmaṇas* and the *Upaniṣads* alike, the supersensuous vision of *Vāk* is the ultimate approach to or experience of the Real. As indicated in passages like *Māṇḍūkya* 3.33, this vision is seen to be a function of the mind in its capacity for direct intuition. Also for the Upaniṣadic *Ṛṣis*, the intuition of the Real has an internal rather than external focus in its symbolic expression. This approach depends for its validity upon the presupposition that the Real is a given truth which requires only to be discovered or revealed. Such a presupposition is held in common by Jainism, Buddhism and the *Ṛṣis* of the *Veda*. It was also accepted by the Greek Philosophers such as Plato. However, this presupposition is currently challenged by various evolutionary and eschatological viewpoints which envision reality to be either a future goal capable of achievement (Marxism, contemporary Christian "Theology of Hope," e.g., Moltmann, or possibly Aurobindo's "Integral Philosophy") or an infinite evolutionary progress or regress in which everything remains phenomenally relative (twentieth century physical and social science). These latter viewpoints would be regarded as merely wrong ideas constructed by the mind which are obstructing the thought and experience of their proponents, so that the true reality is not seen.

Having surveyed the Vedic word or *mantra*, we have seen how the Upaniṣadic Seers sought to unify, interiorize, and give clearer philosophic expression to the common vision of the Real. This approach also depends upon the acceptance of certain presuppositions for validity. The unifying and abstracting tendency assumes an impersonal absolute (such as Divine *Vāk*) to be the highest formulation of the Real. At the same time, the interiorizing approach to the real presupposes that the real is intrinsic in each individual. Consequently, for the *Ṛṣis*, the revealed work (*śruti*) is not the ultimate truth in itself, but serves the *necessary* function of enabling one to "see" ultimate

1. Ka. Up. 6.10 ff.
2. Tait. Up. 2.8 and 9.

reality through its penultimate verbalizations (e.g., the *Mahāvākyas*). Buddhism, as will be shown, objects to all of these approaches to the Real : no scripture is necessary, only one's reason is required; unifying and interiorizing tendencies must be overcome by focusing on the discrete and momentary elements of reality. With regard to the question of a necessary revelation, the approach of the Upaniṣadic Seers seems superior for the reason that within Buddhism the words of the Buddha rapidly were taken to be necessary vehicle by which the direct intuition of the Real could be achieved—filling the function of a necessary revelation. Of course, for both Buddhism and the *Upaniṣads*, the direct face to face vision or intuition of the Real is ultimate—although the two views are in complete opposition as to the nature of the reality that is seen.

In relation to the Brahmanical tradition as a whole, the effects of the approaches[1] adopted by the Upaniṣadic *Ṛṣis* have been described as subordinating the material utility of the *mantra* and the ritual sacrifice to a more purely spiritual aim and intention. In practical terms, this resulted in an increased emphasis upon asceticism and renunciation.[2] In addition to achieving the culmination of the Vedic approach to the divine *Vāk*, these Upaniṣadic *Ṛṣis* also provided the foundations upon which the subsequent schools of the Brahmanical tradition base themselves. Let us now examine how the schools of *Sāṅkhya-Yoga*, *Mīmāṁsā* (although it rejects the *jñāna-kāṇḍa*) and *Vedānta* give more systematic formulation to this *Daivī Vāk* view of language.

Language in the Brahmanical Schools

Before discussing the various views of language as such, it is necessary that the scholastic Indian conceptions of knowledge (*pramā*) and the methods or ways of knowing (*pramāṇa*) be understood, since they underlie all language discussions issuing from the Vedic views of *Vāk*. In Sanskrit the word *jñāna* stands for all kinds of cognition irrespective of the question of truth and falsehood, whereas the word *pramā* is used to designate only a

1. The word "approaches" here has been interpreted in the sense of "methods of drawing near" from the definition given in *The Concise Oxford Dictionary*.

2. Aurobindo, *Veda*, p. 17.

true cognition (*yathārtha-jñāna*) as distinct from a false one (*mithyā-jñāna*). Datta cites the *Vedānta-paribhāṣā* definition or *pramā* or knowledge as "a cognition the object of which is neither contradicted nor already known as an object (*anadhigatābādhitārtha-viṣayaṁ jñānam*)".[1] *Pramāṇa*, according to the same authority, is the special source of particular *pramā*. "Special source" here is described in terms of active and unique causation. Datta describes exactly what is meant as follows :

> In the case of perceptual knowledge or *pratyakṣa pramā*, for example, a sense-organ (in the case of an external perception) or the mind (in the case of an internal perception) is said to be the *kāraṇa* or instrumental cause. There are many causes, e.g, the mind, the sense organ, etc., the existence of which is necessary for the production of perceptual knowledge of an external object. But of these, the mind is a cause the existence of which is common to all sorts of knowledge, perceptual and inferential; so it cannot be regarded as a special cause. The special cause here is the particular sense-organ involved in that perception, because it is not common to other kinds of knowledge; it is peculiar to external perception alone . . .
>
> A *pramāṇa* is, then, such an active and unique cause (*kāraṇa*) of a *pramā* or knowledge.[2]

Let us now briefly note the particular *pramāṇas* accepted by each of the philosophic schools within the Brahmanical tradition. The *Sāṅkhya* and the *Yoga* Schools accept three pramāṇas; *pratyakṣa* (perception), *anumāna* (inference), and *śabda* (testimony).[3] The *Mimāṁsā* defines six *pramāṇas*: *Pratyakṣa*, *anumāna*, *śabda*, *upamāna* (analogy), *arthāpatti* (presumption) and *abhāva* (non-apprehension).[4] The same six *pramāṇas* are also stated by *Vedānta*.[5] Of course there are many differences of

---

1. D. M. Datta, *The Six Ways of Knowing*, p. 27. Hereafter cited Datta, *Six*. On pp. 20-27 Datta examines the differences in interpretation given to *pramā* by the various Indian schools, but concludes that they all essentially agree with the definition quoted above.

2. *Ibid.*, pp. 27-28.

3. See the *Sāṅkhya Kārikā of Īśvara Krishna, Kārikā IV*; *The Sāṅkhya Aphorisms*, I:88, *Yoga Sūtras of Patañjali*, I:7.

4. See Ganganatha Jha, trans., *Pūrva-Mīmāṁsā in Its Sources*, p. 80. Hereafter cited Jha, *Pūrva-Mīmāṁsā*. Prabhākara accepts only five *pramāṇas*.

5. See Dharmarāja Adhvarin, *Vedānta Paribhāṣā*, Chapters 1-6.

definition regarding a specific *pramāṇa* among the schools. Our purpose here is to focus only on the *śabda pramāṇa* and briefly examine the various interpretations offered by the above schools.

Sāṅkhya describes *śabda* as being constituted by authoritative statements (*āptavacana*), and resulting in a knowledge of objects which cannot be known through perception or inference. Two kinds of *śabda* are distinguished—*vaidika* and *laukika*. *Śabda* as *vaidika* is the revelation of the *Vedas*. *Śabda* as *laukika* is the testimony of ordinary trustworthy persons and, according to some authors, is not recognized in the *Sāṅkhya* as a separate *pramāṇa*, since it depends on perception and inference. It is *vaidika śabda* or the *Vedas* which alone give us true knowledge of the supersensuous realities that are beyond perception and inference.[1] This firm division of *śabda*, however, is called into question by the statement of the *Sāṅkhya Aphorisms* that *śabda* as secular is not different from *śabda* as *Veda*.[2] Here *śabda* is defined as the testimony arising from a person worthy to be believed.[3] A recent writer suggests that *vaidika śabda* is used in *Sāṅkhya* primarily with respect not to the *Vedas*, but to the tradition of Sāṅkhyan teachers.[4] Although *Sāṅkhya* formally admits *śabda* as *Veda* as an independent *pramāṇa*, it is inference which is really the chief Sāṅkhyan *pramāṇa*.[5] The attitude of this school would seem to be to keep *śabda* as *Veda* handy to fall back on when inference and perception fail. In this sense Scripture may be said to be subordinate to reason for *Sāṅkhya*.

The *Vedas* are described as not made by any person, therefore free from defects and possessing self-evident validity.[6] They are spontaneously conveyors of right knowledge as a result of their inherent natural power.[7] Although the *Vedas* are impersonal, they are not eternal for, as shown in the previous section, they arise out of the spiritual experiences of *ṛṣis* and are conserved by a continuous line of instruction from generation to

1. See S. C. Chatterjee and D. M. Datta, *An Introduction to Indian Philosophy*, p. 312. Hereafter cited Chatterjee and Datta, *Introduction*.
2. *Sāṅkhya Aphorisms*, V:40.
3. *Ibid*., Bk. I., Aph. 101.
4. G. J. Larson, *Classical Sāṃkhya*, p. 172.
5. *Sāṅkhya Aphorisms*, I:60.
6. See S. Chatterjee, *The Nyāya Theory of Knowledge*, p. 320.
7. *Sāṅkhya Aphorisms*, V:51.

generation.[1] *Vāk* is not eternal in that it evolves from *Ahaṅkāra* according to its own teleology, and expresses itself as sound (this fact is shown to us by inference).[2] The Sāṅkhyan School does not delve into the question of just how *śabda* conveys meaning. It is simply affirmed that the intelligibility of the *Veda* is natural and undeniable.[3] The aim of all Sāṅkhyan thought is the achievement of discriminative knowledge so that the real separation of *puruṣa* from *prakṛti* can be realized and liberation from ignorance achieved. This truth, however, cannot be known from verbal authority or inference but must be directly discerned as an immediate intuition or perception.[4]

Yoga adopts the Sāṅkhyan metaphysics with its three *pramāṇas* of perception, inference and verbal testimony,[5] but in *Yoga* the primary concern is the achievement of a practical psychological technique by which the liberation of the *puruṣa* (as described by *Sāṅkhya*) can be achieved. Verbal testimony, here referred to as *āgama*, is defined as "a thing which has been seen or inferred by a trustworthy person is mentioned by word in order that his knowledge may pass over to some other person."[6] In Vâcaspati's gloss the observation is made that according to this definition the teachings of Manu and other sages would not be judged as *āgama* since they speak of things neither seen nor inferred. But this objection is refuted by noting that as long as such a teaching has been disclosed in the *Veda*, it is *āgama*, for all of the *Veda* was perceived by its original speaker—Īśvara. Truth (*satya*) is described as occurring when word and thought are in accord with the facts that have been seen, heard and inferred. Speech is uttered for the purpose of transferring one's knowledge to another. True speech can only be employed for the good of others and not for their injury.[7]

Perhaps the most noticeable difference between the *Yoga* and *Sāṅkhya* Schools is the high place accorded to Īśvara by the

1. *Sāṅkhya Aphorisms*, V:45-50.
2. *Ibid.*, I:62, V:50.
3. *Ibid.*, V:43, 44.
4. *Ibid.*, I:58, 59.
5. See Y.S., I:7.
6. See James Haughton Woods, Trans., *The Yoga System of Patañjali*. Harvard Oriental Series, Vol. XVII, ed. Charles Rockwell Lanman, pp. 20-21.
7. *Ibid.*, II:30.

former. When the unique universal and eternal superiority, claimed for Īśvara, is challenged, it is interesting to note that the authority of the sacred teachings (*śāstra*) is invoked to prove the contention. When the authority of the scriptures is questioned, a circular argument results :

> The authority (of the śāstra) is the supremacy of His Universal Essence (Īśvara's sattva). These two, the supremacy and the sacred teaching, exist in the Universal Essence of Īśvara eternally related to each other. For this reason does it become possible that He is ever free, and ever the Lord.[1]

Vācaspati's gloss attempts to overcome objections to the circularity of the argument by stating that what the sacred teachings reveal is not a cause and effect relationship but the true correspondence which has existed beginninglessly between the word expressing a meaning (*vācaka*) and the thing expressed (*vācya*). The self-evident validity of this perfect correspondence between *vācaka* and *vācya* constitutes *āgama* or true *śabda pramāṇa*, and is made possible because of the purity of Īśvara's *sattva*. The *śāstra* is taken to be the authoritative distinguishing characteristic of Īśvara.[2]

Yoga elucidates this conception of Īśvara by emphasizing that in Īśvara the seed of omniscience is present in its utmost excellence. By inference it is shown that our process of knowing the supersensuous as it arises out of the past, future or present, either collectively or individually, is possible only through the *āgama*—the verbalization of Īśvara's omniscience, which he has given to us only because of his compassion.[3] This same Īśvara, in his omniscience, is the teacher (*guru*) of the ancient *ṛṣis*, with whom he differs in that they are limited by time while he is not.[4] There is one word which when spoken connotes Īśvara with all his power for omniscience. That is the *praṇava* or the sacred syllable AUM.[5] In his commentary on this *sūtra* Vyāsa

1. See James Haughton Woods, Trans., *The Yoga System of Patañjali*, Harvard Oriental Series, Vol. XVII, ed. Charles Rockwell Lanman, I:24; Vyāsa *Bhāṣya* on Patañjali's *Yogasūtras*, trans. by Rāma Prasāda.

2. *Ibid.*, *Ṭīkā*. All quotations from the *Ṭīkā* are taken from the above translation.

3. *Ibid.*, I:25; See *Bhāṣya* and *Ṭīkā*.
4. *Ibid.*, I:26.
5. See Y.S. I:27.

raises many thorny questions regarding the nature of language. In answer to the question as to whether the relationship between the word and the meaning signified is conventional or inherent, it is stated that the relationship is inherent and self-manifesting. The conventional activity of Īśvara is only for the purpose of manifesting this meaning which is already inherently existing. In other creations, too, this same inherent relation between the word and its meaning existed.[1] Vācaspati's gloss explains the intended meaning as follows :

> All words have the capability of meaning objects of all forms. Their relation with objects of all forms must, therefore, be inherent. And the convention of Īśvara is the determining factor and the shower thereof...[2]

According to the *Yoga* School Īśvara or God repeatedly recreates this same convention in each new creation—it is in this sense that the āgamic words are said to be eternal (but not independently eternal as is held by the *Mīmāṁsā* school). All of the above, says *Yoga*, can only be known through the authority of *śabda pramāṇa* or the *āgama* itself.

Patañjali, having defined the word as possessing inherent power to express meaning, then describes how the yogin is to repeat the *praṇava* (AUM) with the result that the habitual consciousness of the yogin more and more comes to approximate the manifestation of the syllable—Īśvara's pure and omniscient *sattva*. The devotee who is diligent in this devotion not only thereby achieves complete clarity regarding the meaning of all words, but also receives grace from Īśvara, who aids the yogin in the attainment of his yogic trance (*samādhi*) and its end goal.[3] *Yoga* differentiates between the quality of knowledge resulting from *śabda* and that resulting from *samādhi*. Since words of scripture are based upon concepts which take note only of the general characteristics of things, they can never take one to the heart of reality. The same is true of inference and perception which can only know things in their gross forms. Only by intense practice of *samādhi* can the gross obstructions of ordinary consciousness be rooted out and the new consciousness, in which

1. See Y.S., *Bhāṣya*.
2. *Ibid.*, *Ṭīkā*.
3. *Ibid.*, I:28.

all things are known in their essences, become established.[1] Such yogic consciousness can tell by its superior perception the inherent meaning of any word and whether a particular usage of a word is in accord with its true meaning.[2] By this kind of yogic perception of the inherent meaning of words there arises the intuitive knowledge of the cries of all living beings.[3]

Mīmāṁsā maintains that *śabda pramāṇa* is a valid and independent means of knowledge of the supersensuous.[4] *Śabda* (which here stands for the Vedic word) is the chief *pramāṇa* for *Mīmāṁsā*, since it is the sole means for knowing injunctions and prohibitions (*dharma*).[5] The word, its meaning or denotation and the relationship between these two are all judged to be inborn, eternal and therefore not subject to creation by any person (e.g. God).[6] When words come from human sources, there are many reasons why the validity or truth of the words may well be doubted (e.g., trustworthiness of the speaker, his source of information, etc.). If a word does not come from a human source, however, it is not open to such defects and there can be no doubt regarding its impersonal truth. Thus the *Veda* is held to be impersonal, eternal and infallible with regard to all that is supersensuous. An objection is raised, however, against this natural view of language. If what has been said above holds true then each word, by virtue of its "inborn meaning," should be understood by everyone the very first time it is heard. Clearly this is not what happens in experience. When a word is heard for the first time no such inborn relationship as the *Mīmāṁsā* proposes is cognized. It is only when we have heard a word several times that we come to know its meaning. Therefore, the nature of the relationship between the word and its meaning must be conventional and not natural.

Śabara replies to this objection by a detailed examination of the nature of *śabda*. First the word is described by Śabara as a verbal unit composed of a number of letters. For example, the word *gauḥ* (which denotes cow) is the verbal unit made up

---

1. See S. N. Dasgupta, *Yoga Philosophy*, p. 344.
2. Y. S. I:42 and 43.
3. *Ibid.*, III:17.
4. See the Śabara *Bhāṣya* in Jha, *Pūrva Mīmāṁsā*, p. 97.
5. *Ibid.*, *sūtra* 5.
6. *Ibid.*, p. 98.

of the letters g, au and ḥ. In experience people understand "word" to mean the vocable whole which is apprehended by the ear—in this case the verbal unit composed of the letters g, au and ḥ. It may be asked, however, if the meaning of the word is said to come from the composite whole, how is it that these three letters which are individually uttered by the speaker and individually strike the ear of the hearer—how can these individually spoken and perceived letters suddenly be cognized as a whole so that the meaning of the word (the composite letter-unit) is understood ?[1] Śabara answers this objection, and states the *Mīmāṁsā* position as follows :

> What happens is that each component letter, as it is uttered, leaves an impression behind, and what brings about the cognition of the denotation of the word is the *last component letter along with the impressions of each of the preceding component letters.* In actual experience the composite word-unit is never found to be anything entirely different from the component letters; hence there can be no "word" apart from the component letters.[2]

Having defended his contention that *śabda* is a verbal unit composed of a number of letters, Śabara then asks exactly what it is that is denoted by the word—the universal (e.g., the class of "cow") or the individual (e.g., a particular cow possessing unique characteristics) ? This question arises because in experience when the word "cow" is spoken, it brings about the idea of the *universal* or class character which is common to all cows, and yet at the same time "in all actions resulting from the use of the word, it is the *individual* cow that comes in."[3] Following Jaimini, Śabara contends it is the class or universal, and not the individual, that is denoted by the word.[4] To sustain his position, Śabara has to answer the objections of the individualist who maintains that if the word denoted the universal, no action would be possible (since all action requires some individual agent); there would be no words expressive of qualities

1. See the Śabara *Bhāṣya* in Jha, *Pūrva Mīmāṁsā*, p. 99. This objection cited by Śabara is put forward by the Grammarian School, whose *Sphoṭa* Theory is examined in Part II of this work.
2. *Ibid.*, p. 100.
3. *Ibid.*
4. *Ibid.*, See *Mīmāṁsā Sūtras* of Jaimini and the *Bhāṣya* of Śabara, I.3.30-35.

as subsisting in substances (e.g., the "six" in six cows); and there could be no injunction referring to "another" such as is given in the Vedic text "another animal should be brought in."[1] In response to the first point Śabara says that as words denote universals and through these also individuals, therefore there is no dissociation from action.[2] For example, in the injunction "Sprinkle water on the rice," since it is not possible to sprinkle water over the universal denoted by the word "rice," the universal is used here for the purpose of qualifying the object of the action of sprinkling water. Śabara argues in the same fashion regarding the second point. Words expressive of qualities (e.g., "six" in cows) are seen as primarily referring to the universal in that what is denoted is simply the amount of that universal (i.e., cowness) that is required. As for the injunction regarding "another" animal, what is indicated here, says Śabara, is a substitute for the one which has become lost—thus the primary reference is to the universal (i.e., the "cowness" which remains constant over both animals). So, maintains Śabara, it is clear that words such as "cow," etc., primarily denote classes or Universals, yet at the same time secondarily refer by implication to the individual possessed of the generic attribute of cowness.[3] As we shall soon see, the Vedāntins adopt this same viewpoint. The *Nyāya* school, however, effectively challenges this interpretation by holding that in the meaning of a word three aspects are always present : the universal, the individual, and the formal.

The *Mīmāṁsā* doctrine of the word as eternal, infallible, and impersonal has aroused much controversy. How, for example, can the word be held to be eternally unchanging when it is not *always* present in our consciousness; when it seems to cease or grow silent and to require human effort for its production again; and when we hear the same word uttered in varying forms of dialect, accent,. or loudness ? Śabara replies to such questions by saying that what is brought about by human effort is only the making present or manifestation of the already existing word.[4] When the sound of the spoken word is no longer

1. See *Mīmāṁsā Sūtras* of Jaimini and the *Bhāṣya* of Śabara, *sūtra* 32.
2. *Ibid.*, *sūtra* 35.
3. *Ibid.*, p. 90.
4. *Ibid.*, *sūtra* 12.

heard, this is not due to any destruction of the word itself; rather, it is a case of non-perception of the word which remains eternally present. When we think of the great variety of accents, dialects, etc., that exist, it is evident that only on the assumption of an eternally existing and unchanging word could communication between individuals take place. Śabara concludes that all this reasoning only supports the Vedic texts which speak of the word as eternal.[1]

The *Mīmāṁsā's* overriding concern is to safeguard the infallibility of the Vedic injunction as the sole means of knowing *dharma*. The argument this far has shown how words, their meanings and the relation between words and their meanings are all eternal. But a further objection could still be raised by saying that when sentences are considered (and the whole of the *Veda* is in sentence form), neither the sentence nor its meaning, nor the relationship between the two is eternal. This is the case in that since the word-meanings have been shown to be eternal, they must therefore also be mutually exclusive and unable to enter into relation with one another. In the absence of any relation the words cannot be held to form a sentence. To make things more difficult, experience shows that sentences are man-made, imperfect and incapable of conveying their meaning to someone on first hearing.[2] In opposing such a viewpoint Śabara argues that the sentence cannot have any separate meaning entirely apart from the meanings of the words composing it. The meaning of the sentence is comprehended only on the comprehension of the meanings of the component words, and does not result from a distinct unit in the shape of "a group of words" (i.e., the sentence conceived as something over and above the words).[3] The sentence can have no independent meaning apart from the meanings of the words composing it. What happens in the sentence is that each of the component words ceases from activity after having expressed its own meaning, and "the meanings of the words thus comprehended bring about the comprehension of the meaning of

1. See *Mīmāṁsā Sūtras* of Jaimini and the *Bhāṣya* of Śabara, *sūtra* 23.

2. See G. V. Devasthali, *Mīmāṁsā : The Vākya-Śāstra of Ancient India*, pp. 202-3; and Kumārila's presentation of the *Pūrva-pakṣin* position "On the Sentence," *Ślokavārttika*, in Jha, *Pūrva Mīmāṁsā*, pp. 486-504.

3. *Śabara-Bhāṣya*, *sūtra* 25.

the sentence as a whole. Consequently the nature of the sentence is no different from that already shown to be the case for words—it too is eternal. In answer to the charge that the sentence cannot be eternal because it is man-made, Śabara says that while this may be true in regard to sentences about ordinary things in this world, it cannot be true of sentences in the *Veda* which relate to supersensuous things and are author-less.[1]

Having safeguarded the eternality of the sentence as being identical with the eternality of the word, Śabara offers an interesting thought as to how the unified meaning of the sentence results from the comprehension of the meanings of the component words. In *sūtra* 25 it is stated, "In the sentence there is only mention of words with definite denotations along with a word denoting action, and the meaning of the sentence is based upon that."[2] The idea here is that the direct denotation of each word—which consists of the universal—is useless in itself, but becomes useful (as a Vedic injunction requiring action) only when it is qualified by the word in the sentence denoting action. This concept is given full formalization in the Prabhākara view which holds that only the injunction of an action is expressive of meaning and hence valid. Prabhākara holds that words with imperative terminations express the Vedic injunction directly, while other words (e.g., the name of the act enjoined, the person enjoined, etc.) denote things related to that injunction. Thus the true meaning of the Vedic sentences is always found in the injunction and prohibition of action. As to how knowledge of the meaning of such words and sentences originally comes about, Prabhākara maintains that people learn the meaning of words only by watching the usage and activity of older people. One person voices a set of words to another, having the result that the latter person acts in a certain manner. It is clear to the observer, claims Prabhākara, that the words spoken must have been in the form of an injunction to do what the other person has done. If, on the face of it, the words do not appear to lay down any action, then their meaning can be found to depend indirectly upon some

1. *Śabara-Bhāṣya*, *sūtra* 26.
2. *Ibid.*, *sūtra* 25.

injunction.[1] As we shall soon see, this systematic position regarding the meaning of sentences (technically called the *Anvitābhidhāna* Theory) results in two important conflicts. It goes directly against the *Vedānta* view that the meaning of the most important Vedic sentences is found not in the laying down of something to be done, but in the pointing out of certain self-evident truths (e.g., the being of *Brahman*). Secondly, the emphases on the meaning of sentences being learned from the usage of older people opens the way for the objection "how can this be regarded as "eternal" when it is based upon the usage of people ?" This objection will be examined when we consider the *Nyāya* position.

Even within the *Mīmāṁsā* School itself there is no unanimity on the question of how the eternality of the sentence is to be defended. Kumārila, in his *Ślokavārttika*, opposes the *Anvitābhidhāna* theory of Prabhākara according to which the meanings of words can be known only when they occur in injunctive sentences—the meaning of words and sentences can only be understood when seen as related to something which has to be done. In objecting to this view Kumārila points out that even though we only encounter words when they are functioning in a sentence, we are still able to understand the individual meanings of words when taken separately. If this were not so a word learned in one context could not be applied in another context, and the isolated understanding of words must be possible if the experience we have of recognizing the same word in a variety of sentences is to be explained. According to Kumārila, all of this is quite understandable when we view the meaning of the sentence as a linking together of the individual meanings expressed by its words. The sentence has no meaning of its own, independent of words :

> Inasmuch as the meaning of a sentence is always comprehended in accordance with the meaning of the words (composing the sentence),—the fact of the sentence having a qualified (particular) signification cannot point to the fact of the sentence being independent (of the words).

---

1. Prabhākara's view on the meaning of the sentence as summarized by G. Jha, *Ibid.*, p. 120.

> For us, even in the signification of the sentence, the words (composing it) do not lose their significance (potentiality); and it is only because the direct function of the words ends in the signification of their own individual denotations, that we hold the meaning of the sentence to be deduced from the *meanings of the words* (and not from the words directly).[1]

In this view it is solely from the connection among the independently expressed word-meanings, that the meaning of the sentence arises. On hearing a sentence, we first have an understanding of the separate meanings of the words one after another, then these word-meanings are related on the basis of syntactic expectancy (*ākāṅkṣā*), fitness (*yogyatā*) and proximity (*saṁnidhi*) so that the meaning of the sentence as a whole is produced. The process is described as follows : "The individual word-meanings are remembered separately until all the words are heard; then there is a simultaneous cognition of the sentence-meaning in which all the word-meanings are properly related to one another on the basis of *ākāṅkṣā*, *yogyatā* and *saṁnidhi*."[2] The resulting sentence-meaning is something more than just the sum of the word-meanings. The individual word-meanings are verbal (*śabda*) since they are directly produced by the words. The sentence-meaning, however, is not produced directly by the words and therefore is not directly *śabda*, but neither is it non-verbal (*aśabda*). It is verbal in that the intention of the speaker (causally operating via *ākāṅkṣā*, *yogyatā* and *saṁnidhi*), which is conveyed by the words, has not yet ceased to function. Thus the words are seen by Kumārila to be the indirect cause of the sentence-meaning.[3] The unified sentence-meaning is referred to by different terms : sentence-meaning (*vākyārtha*), association (*saṁsarga*) of the word-meanings and the purport or intention of the speaker (*tātparyārtha*).[4] This view of Kumārila,

1. Kumārila, *Ślokavārttika*, trans. Ganganatha Jha, pp. 527-28. Hereafter cited Jha, *Ślokavārttika*.

2. K. Kunjunni Raja, *Indian Theories of Meaning*, p. 208. Hereafter cited Raja, *Theories*.

3. See Jha, *Ślokavārttika*, pp. 527-28. According to Prabhākara's theory, on the other hand, each word, as it is being uttered, contributes to the meaning of the sentence which is revealed step by step, becoming clearer and clearer with the utterance of the subsequent words.

4. See Raja, *Theories*.

called the *Abhihitānvaya* Theory, defends the eternality of the sentence by showing how its meaning arises from the juxtaposition of words, the eternality of which has been proven previously.

On one point the *Mīmāṁsā* School markedly differs from all others in the Brahmanical tradition—its complete rejection of yogic intuition. The Mīmāṁsakas deny the possibility of omniscience of any kind, either eternal as of God, or as a result of *samādhi* as described by Patañjali. After reviewing the *Mīmāṁsā* arguments in support of denial, Gopinath Kaviraj finds them "to be no more than the stale stock-in-trade arguments with which the common empirical sense of man seeks to overthrow the dictates of the higher mystic consciousness."[1] He suggests the real reason behind this denial is their conception of *śabda* as eternal, impersonal, self-revealed and the source of all knowledge. With this high conception of *śabda*, not only would it be superfluous to posit a personal omniscient being, but such knowing via personality (rather than by *śabda*) would open the door to doubting *śabda* since personality is a limitation which inevitably results in the relativity of consciousness, and the impossibility of omniscience and eternality.[2]

Vedānta also accepts *śabda pramāṇa* as a valid and independent means of knowledge of the supersensuous.[3] As in the *Mīmāṁsā*, the *Vedānta* School holds that the word, its meaning, and the relationship between the two is eternal and therefore not subject to creation by any person. *Vedānta* also agrees that *śabda pramāṇa* is vitally important in that it enables one to realize *mokṣa* (freedom or release from suffering). The capacity of *śabda* to give such "saving knowledge" assumes both the immediate apprehension of the meanings of words in a sentence, and the ability to understand the purport of a sentence. The former requires the absence of ignorance or delusion which would obstruct the apprehension of the knowledge inherent in *śabda*. The understanding of the purport of a sentence requires both concentrated study and the application of inference as developed

1. Gopinath Kaviraj, *The Doctrine of Pratibhā in Indian Philosophy*, Annals of the Bhandarkar Oriental Research Institute, 1924, pp. 120-121. Hereafter cited Kaviraj, *Pratibhā*.
2. *Ibid.*
3. *Vedānta Paribhāṣā*, trans. S. S. S. Sastri, pp. 65-88.

by the *Mīmāṁsā* School. The six characteristics of purport are : the harmony of the initial and concluding passages, repetition, novelty, fruitfulness, glorification by eulogistic passages or condemnation by deprecatory passages and intelligibility in the light of reasoning.[1] When the purport of a sentence is both uncontradicted by other *pramāṇas* and unknown through other *pramāṇas*, then that sentence is held to be *śabda pramāṇa* or a valid verbal revelation. From this viewpoint, a false statement results not because of any inadequacy in the words themselves, but because the delusions or ignorance of the person speaking act as an obstacle which prevents the intrinsic truth of the words from being cognized. In the case of a reliable person's statement, however, there are no such obstacles present, and the inherent meaning of the word is clearly cognized by the listener. On this theoretical basis, if it can be shown that there are certain sentences lacking authors, then the knowledge which they give will be free from error; thus the thesis of all the *Brahmanical* Schools that the *Veda* is authorless and eternal. In cases where some *mantra* is said to have been composed by a particular *ṛṣi*, this does not mean than the *ṛṣi* in question created the *mantra* but rather that the *ṛṣi* himself has been generated from the words of the *Veda*. In his commentary on the *Brahma Sūtra*, Śaṅkara says that at the (relative) beginning of each creation (*kalpa*), God, who is self-illumined, creates *Brahmā* and delivers the *Vedas* to him in the same form as they existed in previous creations. With this power *Brahmā* then gives to all the *ṛṣis* who had existed previously their same names and their same vision of the Vedic *mantras*. Just as the various seasons of the year return in succession, so the same seers and *Vedas* appear again in each different creation cycle, so that the *Vedas* of the present are equal in name and form to those of the past.[2] It is in this way that *Vedānta* maintains the impersonality and eternality of the *Veda*, while at the same time suggesting that God is somehow the eternal omniscient author. The argument is

1. T. M. P. Mahadevan, *The Philosophy of Advaita*, p. 57. Hereafter cited Mahadevan, *Philosophy*.

2. Ś. B. B. S. I, 3.30. See George Thibaut, trans., *Vedānta Sūtras with the Commentary by Śaṅkarācārya*. Sacred Books of the East Series, ed. F. Max Müller, XXXIV. All quotations from Ś. B. B. S. are taken from this translation.

similar to the one used by *Yoga* in explaining the eternal co-existence of Īśvara and the *Veda.* Various explanations are offered by *Vedānta* scholars. Vācaspati argues that both *Veda* and God are beginningless, but that God is the ultimate source. Amalānanda explains it as follows : a lamp may be lit by Devadatta, but its ability to give light is its own and not due to Devadatta. Similarly, although God is the cause of the *Veda,* its validity is intrinsic. Referring to the *Chāndogya Upaniṣad* (4.15.1) Śaṅkara argues that the *Veda* itself states that it is but breath of the great Being. As easily as a man exhales, so God produced the *Veda,* as if in play. Due to its self-evident omniscience and omnipotence, nothing but *Brahman* can be inferred as its cause.[1]

Śaṅkara has dwelt upon this issue at some length. He carefully distinguishes between "evolution of the world from *Brahman*" and "evolution of the world from *śabda.*" *Brahman,* he maintains, is the material cause of the world while *śabda* is only an efficient cause. Just as experience shows us that in doing something we first remember the significant words and then act according to those words, so it was that before creation the Vedic words became manifest in the mind of Prajāpati, the creator, and that he created things corresponding to those words.[2] While *śabda* is seen as the efficient cause of creation, however, Śaṅkara takes us a step further to the material cause and originating will which lies behind *śabda*—the mysterious desire of *Brahman* to get into diversity from unity was the direct cause of creation.[3] Or as a contemporary Vedāntin puts it, creation occurs due to a "free phenomenalization" of *Brahman.*[4]

In agreement with the *Mīmāṁsā,* Śaṅkara not only maintains that *śabda* is eternal, but that the connection between the word and what it denotes is also eternal : "...we observe the eternity of the connection between words such as cow, and so on, and the things denoted by them."[5] In the same passage Śaṅkara

1. These arguments and many others on this point are summarized by K. S. Murty, *Reason and Revelation in Advaita Vedānta,* pp. 40-50. Hereafter cited Murty, *Reason.*

2. See Ś. B. B. S. 1.3.28, p. 204.

3. Ch. Up. 4.2.3. and Ś. B. B. S. 1.1.5.

4. T. R. V. Murti, "Unpublished Lectures on *Vedānta,*" McMaster University, (1971/72).

5. Ś. B. B. S., 1.3.28, p. 202.

also accepts the *Mīmāṁsā* argument that it is the universal, rather than the particular, with which the words are eternally connected. Like the *Mīmāṁsā*, Śaṅkara argues that meaning results from the comprehension of an aggregate of letters by the *buddhi*, and not from the manifestation of some mysterious *sphoṭa* by the group of letters as is argued by the Grammarian School.[1] As this debate will provide the focus for Part Two of this study, the issue will not be developed any further at this point.

While discussing the *Mīmāṁsā* School, two opposing theories regarding the nature of the meaning resulting from sentences were noted. The Prābhākaras argued, like many modern pragmatists or instrumentalists, that the words of a sentence necessarily take their meaning from the verb or the action required from the subject (the *Anvitābhidhāna* Theory). Śaṅkara,[2] and his notable disciple Prakāśātman,[3] argue against this theory. They reject the claim that "doing" or the verb is the entire meaning of the sentence and that the performance of injunctions contains the entire meaning and purpose of the *Veda*. This view is antagonistic to the essence of the *Advaita Vedānta*, which champions the Vedic texts holding reality to be attainable through knowledge rather than action, and philosophically holding the absolute to be "being" rather than "becoming."[4] Although there is no complete agreement among Vedāntins on this point, the majority seem to follow Śaṅkara and Prakāśātman and side with the other *Mīmāṁsā* view (Kumārila's interpretation) that the words of a sentence present only their primary isolated meanings. Those meanings then combine under the influence of factors such as expectancy, compatibility, proximity and purport, to produce the particular synthesized meaning of the sentence. According to this view (the *Abhihitānvaya* Theory), nouns as well as verbs have eternal denotations, and, therefore statements of fact, which offer no injunctions, are still significant in that they can indicate the state of reality and thus dispel illusions. Applying this

1. Ś. B. B. S., 1.3.30, p. 210.
2. See Ś. B. B. S., 1.1.4. pp. 36-45.
3. See Prakāśātman, *Śābdanirṇaya*, pp. 50 ff. Hereafter cited Prakāśātman, *Śābdanirṇaya*.
4. See Datta, *Six*, p. 302.

approach the Vedāntin finds that all *śabda* and all *Veda* has the non-dual *Brahman* for its purport.[1] Initially *śabda* and *Veda* are not known like this because of ignorance (*avidyā*). *Avidyā*, however, is not ultimately real and its obstructing or veiling effect may be removed by the achieving of knowledge through the great sentences of the *Veda* (the *mahāvākyas*).[2] In opposition to the *Mīmāṁsā* School, which holds that such sentences regarding *Brahman* are secondary to injunctions, Śaṅkara maintains that the *Vedānta* sentences are ultimate since through them comes the realization of the identity of *Brahman* and one's true Self (*Ātman*). In this way these sentences are held to give knowledge which is unobtainable through any of the other *pramāṇas* such as perception and inference. Therefore, they are said to be independently authoritative.[3] "That Thou art" is one such great text which teaches that the sense of "I" everyone possesses is, in its true nature, identical with *Brahman.* This *mahāvākya* is judged to be the purport of the *Vedas* and therefore the foundation for *Advaita Vedānta.*[4] Once this revelation of absolute oneness is achieved, maintains Śaṅkara, *śabda* and the *Vedas* will have been superseded since *śabda pramāṇa* is meaningful only when one is in the bondage of *avidyā.*[5]

All of the above assumes a concept which is repugnant to all of the *Mīmāṁsā* thinkers. In Sanskrit this concept is variously referred to as "*pratibhā*," "*prajña*," "*anubhava*" and "*śabda-aparokṣya.*"[6] In the *Vedānta* view of *śabda* all these terms refer to the experience of an immediate conscious communion with the Supreme Being or *Brahman* which coincides with the removal of the veil of ignorance by the *mahāvākyas.*[7] "That Thou art,"

1. Prakāśātman, *Śābdanirṇaya*, p. 69.

2. "*Mahāvākya*" literally means "great sentence" and is a term used in *Advaita Vedānta* to refer to the "great sentences" in the *Upaniṣads* that contain the quintessence of the Ultimate Truth as realized by the ancient *ṛṣis*. There are four *Mahāvākyas* : *Tat Tvaṁ Asi* (You are that), *Aham Brahmāsmi* (I am *Brahman*), *Prajñānam Brahman* (Consciouness is *Brahman*), and *Ayam Ātmā Brahma* (This Self is *Brahman*).

3. See Ś. B. B. S., 1.1.4.

4. K. S. Murty, *Reason*, pp. 88-98.

5. Ś. B .B. S., 4.1.3.

6. *Śābdanirṇaya*, defines *śabda-aparokṣya* as "the immediacy of *śabda* knowledge. See Prakāśātman, *Śābdanirṇaya*, pp. 71-72.

7. Gopinath Kaviraj, *Pratibhā*, pp. 116-120; and K. S. Murty, *Reason*, p. 103.

for example, teaches one to recognize the truth which is inherently given. Just as a prince kidnapped by robbers in his childhood does not know that he is a prince, but realizes himself to be a prince as soon as he is told, so also an individual ego (*jīva*) realizes himself to be *Brahman* as soon as he hears the *mahāvākya*. It is via this kind of immediate intuition that *Vedānta* believes supersensuous knowledge to be given by *śabda pramāṇa*. Technical words and proper names are exceptions, however, since their referents are neither eternal nor universally known.

Within the *Advaita Vedānta* School itself there is some difference of interpretation in regard to just how this intuition of word meaning occurs. For example, Prakāśātman says that the word meanings are immediate from the start. Thinking or enquiry into the purport of the sentence (*adhyāsa*) is only required to remove the obstacles of *avidyā*, and does not result in any qualitative change in the meaning which is inherently present from the beginning. On the other hand Vācaspati Miśra regards *śabda pramāṇa* as capable of generating only mediate knowledge. The *mahāvākyas* are first perceived as mediate knowledge and only through continued *adhyāsa* does the sentence meaning become immediate. In this view there is a qualitative change in the meaning achieved. This interpretation is supported by appeal to scriptures such as the *Chāndogya Upaniṣad* where Indra, after knowing mediately the nature of the self as indicated in the text, "That self which is devoid of defect, rid of ravaging effect of age,"[1] etc., approached his teacher four times with the intention of acquiring the intuitive experience of the self.[2] Such differences of opinion regarding the way in which *śabda* achieves immediacy do not detract from the main thrust of the *Advaita* contention—that the pluralistic world of everyday experience cannot be consistently explained without admitting one underlying unity which transcends all diversities, and that this unity can only be known through the intuition of the meaning of the *mahāvākyas* (reports of the direct realization of that fundamental unity by the *ṛṣis*). These authoritative sentences will first be perceived as conveying only mediate

1. Ch. Up., 8.7.1.

2. Vācaspati's view as presented by T. M. P. Mahadevan, *Philosophy*, pp. 58-59. This is the difference between the *Vivaraṇa* and *Bhāmatī* Schools.

knowledge, but as one undergoes the fourfold mental and moral discipline[1] these truths known from *śabda pramāṇa* attain immediacy (*aparokṣatva*). This process is illustrated by the story of the ten persons who, having crossed a river, count themselves. Every time the counter forgets to count himself and finds only nine. They mourn the loss of their tenth comrade. The error is corrected by a passerby who counts all, and tells the counter, "You are the tenth." This mediate knowledge from *śabda* afterwards becomes immediate knowledge when, counting again and including himself, the counter comes to realize "I am the tenth."[2] In a similar way the earnest seeker perceives from the *mahāvākyas* that *Brahman* is the one reality in all outer things and in the inner self, and achieves an immediate consciousness of "I am *Brahman*." Once this revelation is achieved, maintains Śaṅkara, then *śabda* and the *Veda* will have been superseded, since *śabda* is meaningful only when one is in the bondage of *avidyā*.[3] Although it is the only *pramāṇa* by which the liberation of absolute truth may be achieved, *śabda*, even as the *mahāvākyas*, is ultimately seen to be a part of worldly phenomenal diversity (*māyā*) which must be negated if the ultimate absolute unity of *Brahman* is to be realized.[4] The *Mīmāṁsā* refusal to accept any kind of *pratibhā* or immediate intuition was to guard against just such an outcome in which the *Vedas* could be considered transcendable.

---

1. These are the *Sādhanacatuṣṭaya*, the attainment of which, according to Śaṅkara, was a necessary precondition to the full-time monastic quest for the realization of the ultimate *Brahman*. The *Sādhanacatuṣṭaya* are : *nityānitya vastuviveka* (discrimination between the eternal and the non-eternal); *ihāmutrārthaphalabhogavirāga* (the relinquishing of the desire for the enjoyment of the fruits of action either here or hereafter); the acquisition of the powers of concentration (*samādhi*) and endurance (*titikṣā*); *mumukṣutva* (the ardent desire for liberation). See Ś. B. B. S., 1.1.1.

2. Vidyāraṇya, *Pañcadaśī*, trans. Swāmī Swāhānanda, 7:22-27, pp 239-41.

3. Ś. B. B. S., 4.1.3.

4. The *Advaita Vedānta* central tenet of the non-duality of *Brahman* raises many thorny issues when considered in relation to *śabda*. For example, *śabda* is held by Śaṅkara to be eternal. Thus it would seem that there are two eternal entities co-existing, *Brahman* and *śabda*, but this is unacceptable when *Brahman* is defined as "absolute non-duality." Then again it is held that *Brahman* alone is real and that truth is made known by *śabda*. Now, is *śabda* which is evidence for *Brahman* real or unreal ? If it is real, then there is a reality other than *Brahman*. If it is unreal, then *Brahman* which is its content cannot be real. For the Advaitin such dilemmas are resolved by holding that, on the phenomenal side, there are various levels in our perception of truth. Ultimately, however, non-dual *Brahman* is the only absolute, and the unreality of *śabda* is accepted. For further discussion of these scholastic arguments, see D. M. Datta, *Six*, K. S. Murty, *Reason*, and T. M. P. Mahadevan. *Philosophy*.

Chapter Three

LANGUAGE IN THE NATURALISTIC TRADITION

In opposition to the high evaluation given language in the Brahmanical tradition, the naturalistic tradition tends to view language as an arbitrary and conventional tool. The validity of *śabda* and *Veda* is denied as a source of knowledge. Professor T. R. V. Murti finds the *Cārvāka* and earlier Buddhism to be representatives of this tradition, while the "empiricistic" *Jaina* and *Nyāya* Schools occupy a somewhat intermediary position.[1]

Like the Brahmanical viewpoint, the naturalistic tradition may be traced back to the *Upaniṣads* and early hymns of the *Vedas*. In his review of the naturalistic tradition of Indian thought, Riepe finds in the *Ṛgveda* "some important assertion of a naturalistic approach to life."[2] He admits, that there is no strong case to be made for the presence of a presystematic naturalism in the *Vedas*, but he does find evidence that attitudes of skepticism, hedonism and materialism were present in hymns such as the "hymn of Creation" (*Ṛgveda* X.129), and maintained in the *Upaniṣads* by sages such as Uddālaka, the great opponent of the *ṛṣi* Yājñavalkya. Riepe feels that Uddālaka may be dated at 640-610 B.C. and is likely earlier than the *Cārvāka* or any of the first systemizations of a naturalistic school in India. He describes Uddālaka's position as follows :

> The point of view represented by Uddālaka appears to have been that of the Breath-Wind Magicians who held, as opposed to their idealistic opponents, that the breath rather than thought or words was the most important element of the human being; briefly, a distinction between holding *stuff* rather than *thought* to be primary. Of such Breath-Wind Magicians who foreshadow the later clear-cut naturalistic outlook, there are at least eighteen among the one hundred thinkers mentioned in the oldest Upaniṣads.[3]

1. See T. R. V. Murti, "Some Thoughts."
2. Dale Riepe, *The Naturalistic Tradition in Indian Thought*, p. 26. Hereafter cited Riepe, *Naturalistic*.
3. *Ibid.*, p. 28.

The step from the early naturalism represented by Uddālaka to the *Cārvāka* School is of considerable importance since "in the *Cārvāka* we have the first and possibly only unquestionable materialistic system in early India."[1]

Cārvāka

The *Cārvāka* School rejects *śabda pramāṇa* as completely false and accepts only the *pramāṇa* of perception as producing true knowledge. Sacred scriptures, religious injunctions, etc., are all considered useless. Everything is held to be derived from material elements (*mahābhūta*) which are judged to possess their own immanent life force (*svabhāva*). Intelligence, thought and words are all seen as derived from these elements. There is no God, no supernatural, no immortal soul, and the only aim of life is to get the maximum of pleasure.[2]

Śabda pramāṇa is rejected by the *Cārvāka* on the grounds that it must first be established by other verbal testimony resulting in an infinite regress unless at some point there is an appeal to direct sensory experience. In addition to this logical reason for rejection *Cārvāka* also holds that *śabda* is unacceptable on epistemological grounds—that it is impossible for perceptual knowledge to be communicated. The argument offered here is that a man knows only what he perceives, and not what someone else says he has perceived.[3] In this view the only referents are material, and direct sensory perception of such material referents is the only valid knowledge of reality.

Early Buddhism

Whereas for the *Cārvākas* sense perception was the only valid knowledge and pleasure produced by sensation the only goal, Buddha taught that "sense knowledge is considered to be inextricably bound up with feeling and desire, and hence is to be eliminated as far as possible because by its nature it is a stumbling block to the ultimate aim of the Buddha, the elimination of

1. Riepe, *Naturalistic*, p. 32.
2. Mādhava Āchārya, *Sarva-Darśana-Saṅgraha*, trans. E. B. Cowell and A. E. Gough, pp. 2-11. All quotations from S. D. S. are taken from this translation.
3. Riepe, *Naturalistic*, p. 66.

craving through understanding or illumination."[1] For the early Buddhists (e.g., the *Theravādins*) intuition is the highest source of knowledge. This intuition (*prajñā*) is defined as "knowledge of things as they are in themselves as distinguished from what they appear to us."[2] Such knowledge is considered to be the only means to freedom or salvation. This Buddhist concept seems virtually parallel to the Yoga concept of intuition which was discussed earlier. *Prajñā* is frequently conceived as an omniscient eye. Buddha, for example, was said to have gained such a divine eye on the memorable night of his overthrow of the demon Māra. Through it he saw the entire knowable reality as if it were reflected in a clear mirror.[3] Only such knowledge gained through one's own experience of intuition is considered to be valid. Sense experiences, words, inferences, etc., are worthwhile only as they help one to overcome the obstacles of ordinary experience, and achieve *prajñā* for oneself. But, in themselves, *śabda*, sense perception, inference, etc., cannot be considered to give knowledge.

It is for this reason that Buddha rejected the Brahmanical claims as to the authority of the *Veda* and its status as *pramāṇa*. The Vedic *ṛṣis*, he claimed, had no direct personal knowledge of the truth of the *Veda*.[4] But, as was pointed out in the previous section of this chapter, such personal knowledge is precisely what was claimed by the *ṛṣis*. This contention of Buddha, therefore, was virtually a denial that the *ṛṣis* were competent persons whose testimony could be trusted. Aside from this, it seems clear that Buddha's intention was not to discredit all *śabda* as incapable of conveying truth, but to show that the truth or falsity of any statement is to be judged by factors other than its claim to be reliable report, self-evident, or authoritative revelation. As Jayatilleke puts it, Buddha's criticism "seems to presuppose that it is possible to determine the veracity of all the assertions by other means than that of revelation, etc., in sofar as it is stated that what is accepted as reliable may prove

---

1. Riepe, *Naturalistic*, p. 127.
2. See Kaviraj, *Pratibhā*, p. 122.
3. *Ibid.*, p. 126.
4. K. N. Jayatilleke, *Early Buddhist Theory of Knowledge*, p. 183. Hereafter cited Jayatilleke, *Early Buddhist*.

in fact to be true or false."[1] In spite of the fact that his followers tended to make Buddha's words into the very kind of absolute authority he was rejecting, it seems clear that Buddha's view was that his own teachings and the path to freedom contained therein were only to be accepted *provisionally* by the disciple until found to be truth in his own direct experience (*prajñā*). Jayatilleke points out that this approach bears some similarity to the attitude of those sceptics who likewise suspend judgment when confronted with statements which may be true or false, but radically differs from it, "in view of the possibility, positively entertained, of knowing whether these propositions were in fact true or false *in this life itself*."[2]

In general, the thrust of the Buddhist criticism of the Brahmanical viewpoint seems aimed more towards discrediting the unquestioning acceptance of a handed down tradition, rather than towards the rejection of *śabda* as having any possibility for truth bearing. Buddha is said to have compared the generations of Vedic teachers to a string of blind men clinging one behind the other in succession. Just because a succession of teachers or teaching is unbroken is no guarantee of its truth.[3] It is perhaps partly in response to this criticism of the early Buddhists that the *Mīmāṁsā* School developed the *apauruṣeya* theory, which makes *śabda* impersonal, eternal, and therefore free from the corrupting influences of personality and ill-remembered transmission as alleged by the Buddhists. In addition to this there is the *Vedānta* claim that not only is *śabda apauruṣeya* but its truth is necessarily realizable by experience (*anubhava*) in this life if one is to achieve salvation. This further interpretation by *Vedānta* would seem to satisfy the requirements for Buddha for confirmation in intuition and at the same time safeguard the Brahmanical claim that *śabda* (and *Veda*) is *pramāṇa*. Buddha's reply to this would likely be that while the study of the *Vedas* may lead to the intuition of truth, this is not necessarily so. One who does not hear the *Veda* but follows the path of moral living and inner concentration, as pioneered by Buddha, can have intuition of truth in the absence of *śabda*.

---

1. Jayatilleke, *Early Buddhist*, p. 185.
2. *Ibid.*
3. *Ibid.*, p. 194.

It has frequently been suggested that the early Buddhist attitude towards *śabda pramāṇa* is two-faced : rejecting it in regard to other schools but accepting it in regard to the teachings and omniscience attributed to Buddha. However, after critically reviewing such claims[1] Jayatilleke persuasively concludes :

> . . . The attitude to authority recommended by the Buddha is not contradictory to and is in fact compatible with the attitude recommended by the Buddha towards his own statements. . . .
>
> The sermons to Kālāma and Bhaddāli . . . *do* state that no statements should be accepted on authority because it is possible that such statements may turn out to be either true or false. . . . Where 'a fellow-monk claims the highest knowledge, one should neither accept what he says nor reject it but without acceptance or rejection should question him' in order to test the veracity of his statement...
>
> This is just what Buddha seems to demand from his own hearers regarding his own statements. He does not want his own statements accepted or rejected but seems to demand that they be tested and accepted if found to be true and presumably rejected if they are found to be false.[2]

As suggested earlier, the teachings and path of Buddha are to be provisionally accepted on faith by the devotee until his own experience leads him to confirm or reject it.

It appears that some time after the death of Buddha there was an authoritative collection of Buddha's teachings; but "authoritative" here refers to the fact that these are the authentic teachings (against which all other texts claiming to be Buddha's words must be compared), and not to any truth claim of the teachings themselves.[3] The criterion for truth, as it was for the *Cārvākas*, is direct empirical perception. But where the Buddhists (and, as we shall see, the *Jainas*) differ from the *Cārvākas* is that the range of empirical perception is extended into what is usually referred to as the extrasensory realm; and just as the *Cārvāka* will allow for knowledge to result from inductive inferences on the data of sensory perception, so the Buddhists

1. Jayatilleke, *Early Buddhist*, pp. 376-401.
2. *Ibid.*, p. 390.
3. *Ibid.*, p. 401.

claim knowledge on the basis of inductive inferences on the data of extrasensory perception.[1] Such extrasensory perceptions are not considered to be miraculous but simply the normal result of the natural development of the mind until the state of *pratibhā* is achieved.

Jaina

Whereas the *Cārvākas* and the early Buddhists both deny *śabda* as an authoritative source of knowledge and therefore may be clearly taken to represent the Naturalistic tradition, Murti points out that in the cases of the Jainas and the *Nyāya* the same clear-cut distinction cannot be maintained. Within Murti's categorization, the Jaina and *Nyāya* are placed in intermediary positions between the two traditions. However, because of their more dominant empiricism, they are included under "the Naturalistic tradition" classification for purposes of discussion.[2]

According to Jaina epistemology consciousness is the inherent essence of every self. This consciousness is not, as the *Cārvākas* hold, a mere accidental property arising only under certain conditions. Nor is it a centreless stream of flux, as advocated by the Buddhists, for it is the essence of a continuing individual self or *jīva*. Consciousness is characterized as being like the sun's light, self-evident, and capable of manifesting all objects unless some obstruction (the physical presence of karmic impurity) prevents it from reaching its object.[3] Once all obstacles are removed the self is omniscient, an achievement which is potential in every self. Body, senses and mind are all constituted by *karmas* or physical impurities and the self's omniscience is limited by them. On the basis of these assumptions, the Jainas suggest a twofold classification of knowledge into immediate and mediate (*aparokṣa* and *parokṣa*).[4] What is ordinarily taken as immediate (e.g., sensuous perception) is held to be merely relatively immediate. Only when the medium of the sense organs is removed does the fully immediate knowledge of the self's inherent knowledge manifest itself. Such a state is one of absolute

1. Jayatilleke, *Early Buddhist*, p. 459.
2. See T. R. V. Murti, "Some Thoughts," p. 8.
3. See Chatterjee and Datta, *Introduction*, p. 86.
4. *Ibid.*

knowledge or omniscience and is called *kevala-jñāna*. We have seen that this kind of absolute omniscience, while acceptable to the *Sāṅkhya*, *Yoga* and *Vedānta*, is rejected by the *Mīmāṁsā* on the basis that it exceeds the limits of personal perception and cognition (through the senses and mind as ordinarily known). This *Mīmāṁsā* objection is bypassed by the Jainas who agree that ordinary knowledge resulting from sense organs and the mind is incapable of omniscience, but that once these physical karmic obstacles are removed the self is capable of knowing all sensory and supra-sensory objects simultaneously so that even the limitations of time and place are superseded.[1]

With this background we are now in a position to understand the Jaina view of *śabda*. *Śabda* is considered *pramāṇa* but is classed, along with inference, as only mediate or non-perceptual knowledge.[2] The knowledge produced by the word of a reliable person and which is not inconsistent with the evidence of perception is called authority, verbal testimony, or *śabda*. A reliable person is defined as one "who knows the object as it is and describes it as he knows it. He who possesses right knowledge and makes a right judgment is said to be reliable or *āpta*."[3] For these reasons he is taken as "authority" and his word is known as testimony. The testimony of *śabda* is held by the *Jainas* to be of two kinds. It is called secular testimony (*laukika*) when the words come from an ordinary reliable person of the world (e.g., one's father). It is called scriptural testimony (*śruta-jñāna*) when it proceeds from a self liberated from the bondage of the karmic senses and mind and who is therefore omniscient. (e.g., Mahāvīra).[4]

The *Jaina Prabhācandra* defines a word as an independent aggregate of letters which are dependent on one another.[5] The way in which a word gives meaning is held to be a result of both its natural capacity for signifying, on the one hand, and the practice of convention, on the other. Regarding the debate as to whether the word denotes the universal or the particular, the Jaina view is that words denote both at the same

1. M. L. Mehta, *Outlines of Jaina Philosophy*, p. 101.
2. *Ibid.*, p. 105.
3. *Ibid.*, p. 113.
4. *Ibid.*
5. As quoted by J. Sinha, *Indian Psychology : Cognition*, I, p. 444.

time. Since objects as they exist are neither universal only nor particular only, so also words denoting objects are not one side only but invoke both aspects together. If, says the Jaina, a word denoted its object in its universal character and lacking any of its particular characteristics, then its object would be unreal since there is no universality without distinctive particular characteristics. *Śabda*, therefore, denotes both the universal and the particular characteristics of an object. In addition to this, Jainas view the positive word as having a negative or excluding function. The word "jar," for example, denotes the object jar but at the same time negates or excludes other objects, such as "cloth." For the Jaina, therefore, *śabda* denotes a many-sided object with its universal and particular characteristics, and its positive and negative characteristics.[1]

Nyāya

Like the Jaina, the *Nyāya* School holds that *śabda* is the teaching of a reliable person, and that it is a *pramāṇa*. As the only means of expressing knowledge is through a sentence, *śabda* as testimony occurs in the form of a group of words syntactically and significantly connected. As long as the meanings of the words composing the sentence are known, then the meaning of the sentence will be known as it is heard. Thus the cause of understanding relating to *śabda* is the knowledge of the meanings of words and not the referent object and its qualities.[2] The *Nyāya* opposes the Prabhākara *Mīmāṁsā* contention that *śabda* must take the form of an injunction, and agrees with both Kumārila and Śaṅkara in maintaining that sentences conveying informative knowledge are also *śabda*.

Just as the Jaina is a realist, so also is the *Nyāya* in his theorizing that the objects of reality exist independent of any knowing mind. Knowledge, therefore, is simply the discovery by a conscious mind of the objects already existing. "Just as the light of a lamp reveals or shows physical things, so knowledge manifests

---

1. J. Sinha, *Indian Psychology* : *Cognit on*, I. p. 445. As noted by Sinha, this interpretation of *śabda* is consistent with the *syādvāda* (sevenfold disjunction) which is the necessary logical complement of the Jaina *anekāntavāda* (not one pointed) doctrine that no one view of reality can be absolute.

2. See K. S. Murty, *Reason*, p. 223.

all objects that come before it'."[1] *Śabda* is one of the four sources of true knowledge. The others are *pratyakṣa* (perception), *anumāna* (inference) and *upamāna* (comparison). The adjective "true" in regard to knowledge is used advisedly, since according to the *Nyāya*, there can be false knowledge. Knowledge is said to be false when it does not correspond to the nature of its given object; and, true when it does correspond to the nature of its object. In answer to the question as to how correspondence to the true nature of the object is to be judged, *Nyāya* replies that the test of the truth or falsity of knowledge is the success or failure of our practical activities in relation to the object. The following example is offered. Wanting to add more sugar to your tea, you take some from the cup before you and stir it into your tea. The tea now tastes sweeter than before and you know that your previous perception of sugar was true. It may happen, however, that you come upon a cup filled with a white powdered substance and, taking it to be sugar, place a pinch of it into your mouth only to discover to your dismay that it is not sugar but salt. In this way it is shown that true knowledge leads to successful practical activities while false knowledge ends in failure and disappointment. The *Nyāya* School concludes therefore, "that the truth of knowledge is not self-evident in it, but is evidenced or known by inference from successful activity."[2] By successful activity they mean that the expected result, arising from the knowledge claimed, is empirically experienced. This approach is common to the *Jainas*, Buddhists, and *Vaiśeṣikas*.[3]

Following the above epistemology, the *Nyāya* takes *śabda* as neither impersonal nor self-evidently valid. It maintains that the *Vedas* are created by God, and that, notwithstanding such divine authorship, their validity ultimately must be proven by perception or inference.[4]

---

1. S. C. Chatterjee and D. M. Datta, *Introduction*, p. 191.
2. S. Chatterjee, *The Nyāya Theory of Knowled* p. 80. Hereafter cited Chatterjee, *Nyāya*.
3. In this representative survey of the various views of *śabda*, the *Vaiśeṣika* School is not included since its focus is on "cosmology" rather than "epistemology." While certain *Vaiśeṣika* scholars seem to treat *śabda* as *pramāṇa* (e.g. Kaṇāda), others reduce it to a form of inference (e.g., Praśastapāda). See summary by K. S. Murty, *Revelation and Reason in Advaita Vedānta*, op. cit., pp. 222-23.
4. S. Chatterjee, *Nyāya*, p. 380.

Nyāya classifies all knowledge from *śabda* under two headings : *dṛṣṭārtha* or that relating to sensuous objects, and *adṛṣṭārtha* or that relating to supersensuous objects. Chatterjee differentiates the two terms as follows :

> Under the first head we are to include the trustworthy assertions of ordinary persons, the saints, and the scriptures insofar as they bear on the perceptible objects of the world. Thus the evidence given by witnesses in law courts, the knowledge about plants that we get from a reliable farmer, the scriptural injunctions about certain rites . . . are illustrations of *dṛṣṭārtha śabda*. The second will include all the trustworthy assertions of ordinary persons, saints, prophets and the scriptures insofar as they bear on supersensible realities. Thus the scientist's assertions about atoms . . . the prophet's instruction about virtue and vice, the scriptural texts on God, heaven, future life and the like are all illustrations of *adṛṣṭārtha śabda*.[1]

Although Chatterjee admits that there is not complete agreement among the later *Naiyāyikas* to the above classification by Vātsyāyana, he maintains that in respect of truth all agree that there is no difference between the trustworthy assertions of an ordinary person, a saint, a prophet and the scriptures as revealed by God.

The *Nyāyas* define *śabda* as word or a particular group of sounds or letters arranged in a fixed order which stands for some thing or idea. The meaning of a word is seen to consist in its relation to the object which it signifies. Consequently, a word may have different meanings according to the different ways in which it may be related to an object. The *Nyāyas* find three different kinds of relation : *abhidhā*, *paribhāṣā*, and *lakṣaṇā*.[2] *Abhidhā* refers to the primary meaning of a word. The relation between the primary meaning and the word may be either direct or indirect. If direct it leads immediately from the word to the knowledge of its meaning. Such a direct relation may be either eternal or non-eternal. When eternal it is called *śakti*

1. S. Chatterjee, *Nyāya*, pp. 318-319.

2. This discussion of the *Nyāya* view of the nature of "word" and its three relations is based on Chatterjee's discussion, *ibid.*, Chp. 18. For an excellent recent evaluation of the Buddhist and the Nyāya viewpoints see B. K. Matilal, *Epistemology, Logic, and Grammar in Indian Philosophical Analysis*.

or the inherent potency of the word (e.g., relation between the word "jar" [*ghaṭa*] and the object called *ghaṭa* is a direct and eternal relation called *śakti*). The *Naiyāyikas* maintain that this eternal *śakti* is due to God's volition which ordained that the particular fixed order of letter sounds *ghaṭa* should mean the object now called *ghaṭa*. Thus, for the *Naiyāyikas*, the meaning of a word even at its most primary level is judged to be conventional (i.e., established by the will of God), and not natural as was maintained by the Schools of the Brahmanical tradition, especially the *Mīmāṁsā*.

Paribhāṣā refers to the non-eternal or changeable relation between a word and its meaning when that convention is established by man rather than God. Proper names and technical terms are examples of this type.

The third kind of relation, *lakṣaṇā*, refers to the secondary meaning of a word. It is the indirect or implied meaning which must be assumed (when the *abhidhā* or primary meaning does not make sense) in order that the word will fit into the context in which it is found. For example, in the sentence "the house is on the Ganges," the word "Ganges" is taken in its secondary meaning of "the bank of the Ganges" rather than its primary meaning of "the stream of water."

After reviewing the many ways in which we come to learn the meanings of words (e.g., from grammar and dictionaries, from perception and comparison, and from the usage of elders), the *Naiyāyikas* conclude that the very profusion of different ways of coming to know the meanings of words proves that the relation between words and their meanings is not natural (as the Brahmanical tradition declares) but conventional. If there were a natural relation fixed between a word and its meaning, as exists for example between fire and burning, then the word should have always co-existed with its referent and that given relation should be known simply by perception. But the word "fire" does not co-exist with the object "fire" and produce any burning sensation in us when we speak the word. Further evidence for the conventional nature of the word is the fact that the same word is used by different people with different meanings.

In answer to the question as to whether the word primarily refers to the particular or the universal in its meaning, the *Naiyāyikas* reject three other views : the Sāṅkhyan contention that a word denotes a particular object; the Jaina view that a word includes both the universal and the particular as a particular form or configuration of component parts; and the argument of the *Mīmāṁsā* and *Vedānta* Schools which maintain that the word really refers to the universal or class character of the individuals. According to the *Naiyāyikas* the correct answer is that a word means all three of these, i.e., the particular, the configuration and the universal. As Chatterjee puts it :

> . . . words do not mean universals only, since these cannot be understood apart from the individuals and their particular forms. A genus can be recognized only through the individuals that constitute it and their peculiar configurations.[1]

All three factors are held to be present in the meaning of a word, although not always occupying the same degree of prominence. Whichever one we are interested in for the moment receives emphasis. For example, when we are searching for difference between things then the individuality aspect in the meaning of the word will be emphasized. The same thing applies to the other two aspects. This may be put more concisely by saying that there are three aspects in the meaning of a word, namely, a pictoral, a denotative, and a connotative. A word calls up the form, denotes the individual and connotes the universal.[2,3]

---

1. B. K. Matilal, *Epistemology, Logic, and Grammar in Indian Philosophical Analysis*, p. 331.
2. *Ibid.*, p. 332.
3. It is relevant at this point to make brief reference to the long and famous debate between the *Nyāya-Vaiśeṣika* and the Buddhist Dignāga schools regarding the universal aspect. The Buddhists reject the idea that there can be some universal characteristic which resides in common in a number of unique particulars. Nor do they accept the possibility of any common entity residing in them. It might be asked, however, how do we have this notion of commonness with reference to the many particulars of a class? The Buddhist maintains that this notion is caused not by a positive commonness residing in all the individual objects of a class, but by the negative commonness which belongs to all the individual objects of a particular class. In the case of cows, for example, the negative commonness is evidenced, says the Buddhist, in that they are all different from the non-cows, viz. horses, etc. Thus the universal aspect of "cowness," according to the Buddhist, is not an external reality, but only a negation in the form of the exclusion of non-cows. The technical term used for this "negative commonness" is *apoha*, which is the Buddhist counterpart of the universal aspect of the realist *Nyāya*

Chatterjee observes that Indian logic leaves no room for the so-called "non-connotative terms" of Formal Logic as claimed by the West.

Dealing with the question as to how the unity of a word is cognized from the perception of its individual letters, the *Nyāya* answers as follows. Since we perceive only one thing at one instant, the individual letters cannot be perceived simultaneously and must therefore be perceived successively. But how can there be a synthesis of these successive perceptions into one word ? According to the *Nyāya* it is by memory. As we perceive the successive letters c-o, traces of each letter are left in our mind. On the perception of the w, aided by the memory of the two preceding letters, the word cow as a whole is cognized and its meaning understood according to convention. Aside from the last clause (meaning being understood according to convention), this *Nyāya* view is in accord with the *Vedānta* and *Mīmāṁsā* theories. However, it contains certain inherent difficulties. Since the *Nyāyas* agree that there can never be more than one cognition, perception or image to be in the mind at one time, how can individual letters be synthesized into a unity when they are remembered if the memory is still individual? To answer this difficulty the Grammarian School proposes the *Sphoṭa* theory which we study in detail in Part II.

The *Nyāya* understanding of how *śabda* gives meaning in sentences seems to differ very little from the *Mīmāṁsā* and *Vedānta* view discussed above. Chatterjee states, "The *Nyāya*, *Mīmāṁsā* and *Vedānta* Schools all adhered to the *abhihitānvaya* doctrine."[1] Perhaps the main notable addition is that the meaning conveyed by a sentence must be determinative knowledge. Determinative knowledge is here defined as the

---

School. D. N. Shastri compares the two views as follows. "Whether the universal is considered to be positive and real according to the realist, or negative and unreal according to the Buddhist, its function is admitted to be two-fold by both of them, viz., (i) inclusion of the common objects of a class, and (ii) exclusion of the objects belonging to all other classes. The realist lays more emphasis on the positive aspect declaring the universal to be an objectively real entity. The Buddhist, however, insists on the negative aspect and describes the universal as a mere mental construction which is objectively unreal." D. N. Shastri, *Critique of Indian Realism*, p. 368.

1. See S. Chatterjee, *Nyāya*, p. 341.

knowledge of a thing as qualified by an attribute. Thus for the *Nyāya* the presence of a verb is not necessary for a sentence, rather it is the presence of "something to be related to something else as substantive to adjective."[1] The meaning of a sentence therefore is the relation it expresses between a substantive and an adjective.

See S. Chatterjee, *Nyāya*, p. 345, example of a sentence of this type : "A fiery hill" or "A red colour."

CHAPTER FOUR

LANGUAGE IN THE *SPHOṬA* APPROACH

Against the above background of the Brahmanical and the Naturalistic traditions, let us now outline the *Sphoṭa* theory of the Grammarians and the particular merits claimed for it.

We have seen that for the Brahmanical thinkers *śabda* is both a valid source of knowledge and the means by which such knowledge may be communicated to others as verbal testimony. Emphasizing this latter function the early Grammarians Pāṇini and Patañjali describe *śabda* primarily in terms of the spoken word or speaking itself (*Vāk*).[1] In the first verse of his *Mahābhāṣya*, Patañjali defines the word as "That on the utterance of which there is common understanding regarding objects (*saṁpratyaya*)."[2] This definition of *śabda* does not intend the identification of the word with the physiological production of speech. As Murti has pointed out the distinction between word (*śabda*) and sound (*dhvani*) is basic to the understanding of language in all Schools of Indian Philosophy. To take the physical sound as the word is to confuse entities of two different orders, like the confusion of the soul with the body. "The word, like the soul, has a physical embodiment in the sound and is made manifest through the latter, but the conveyance of meaning is the function of the word; the sound only invokes the word."[3] If the word, or *śabda*, is only manifested and not constituted by the vocal sounds or *dhvani*, the question then arises as to the exact nature of this *śabda* which is manifested. We have seen according to the Naturalistic Schools, that just as we create names for our children and various discoveries and so initiate new conventions, the origination of all words should be understood in a similar way. In this way of thinking all words are the result of convention. Where human convention is not allowable, the divine convention of God may be invoked—as is

1. See S. D. Joshi, *Patañjali's Vyākaraṇa-Mahābhāṣya*, p. vi.
2. T. R. V. Murti, "Some Thoughts," p. 10.
3. *Ibid.*, p. 11.

done by the *Nyāya*, for example. Against this view, the Grammarians support the Brahmanical Schools, especially the *Mīmāṁsā*, in their contention that words and their relation with meaning are eternal, underived and impersonal. The relation between *śabda* and its meaning is not an arbitrary convention established by either man or God or both. Not only is there no record of any such convention, but the very idea of "convention" itself presupposes language—the very thing claimed to be derived from convention. Murti makes the point quite clear :

> To make conventions, words have to be used and understood by persons participating in the convention. This is clearly circular. Invoking God does not help either. How could God make known his intentions, his conventions between words and their respective meanings to persons who did not use language already ?[1]

It would seem, therefore, that language must be taken as having existed beginninglessly; or, as somehow being co-eternal with God (as suggested by the *Yoga* School and in the Christian tradition by Chapter One of the *Gospel of John*). As Murti suggests, the attempt to discover a temporal beginning of language may arise from a confusion of the *śabda* with *dhvani*. While speaking sounds and learning how to group sounds into syllables, etc., may well be conventional, the fact of verbal communication necessitates the acceptance of *śabda* as a given which the learned spoken sounds manifest, but do not constitute. Here the viewpoint of the Grammarians and the Brahmanical tradition seems very similar to the Platonic concept of the universality and eternity of the idea. Whereas in Platonic doctrine the relation of the idea to the "copies" is described as the relation of the immutable to its several manifestations, here the word is the immutable which is first perceived through its several physical manifestations.[2] The word "go" ("cow"), for example, is a word-form which is identical and immutable although its physical manifestations may differ markedly with regard to accent, speed of speaking, place and time of utterance, etc. But the Grammarians go further than just establishing the

1. T. R. V. Murti, "Some Thoughts," p. 12.
2. *Ibid.*, p. 14.

eternality of *śabda*. They identify *śabda* with the *Brahman*—all words ultimately mean the Supreme *Brahman*. The meaning intended by this absolutistic claim is described as follows :

> ...Brahman is the one object denoted by all words; and this one object has various differences imposed upon it according to each particular form; but the conventional variety of the differences produced by these illusory conditions is only the result of ignorance. Non-duality is the true state; but through the power of "concealment" [exercised by illusion] at the time of the conventional use of words a manifold expansion takes place...[1]

On this basis knowledge of the meaning of words not only abolishes ignorance but also leads to the final bliss of identity with *Brahman*.

In our discussion of the two traditions above, we have seen various positions taken on the issue of whether *śabda* signifies its meaning through the universal or through the particular. Indian language speculation appears to contain a vast variety of views ranging from the extreme nominalism of the Buddhist to the realism of the *Mīmāṁsā* and the *Nyāya*. On this question the School of Grammar offers two views. In the *Vākyapadīya*, Bhartṛhari first makes clear that the real unit of language is the sentence, and that for pedagogical purposes words are abstracted from the sentence and ascribed a meaning. Thus the idea that words are divided into syllables and sentences into words is "a convenient fiction."[2] According to the one view suggested by the School of Grammar, the word-meaning is connotated by the universal. As Murti puts it, "The universal is primarily a Word-Form and by way of transference this is applied to the Idea-Universal."[3] The particulars are merely the appearances of the universal. For practical purposes we may speak of several universals such as man, cow, horse, etc., but in the final analysis there is only one ultimate universal-being, and it is this that all words mean. This view is by its logic identical to the *Advaita Vedānta* position which, as was shown, holds in all things for the non-duality of the Real and

1. S. D. S., "The Pāṇini Darśana," p. 219.
2. T. R. V. Murti, "Some Thoughts," pp. 14-15.
3. *Ibid.*

the appearance and defines the relationship as a one-sided dependence upon the Real. The other view suggested by the School of Grammar is that the meaning is to be found in the individual object the word denotes. Here substance or the substantive being of the particular is taken as the thing which remains permanent throughout the changes. Meaning on this view, says Murti, is denotation—the *that* of things.[1] Ultimately, of course, there is still one indivisible being which is the meaning of all individual words. In this case the individuals are seen as appearances which exist through limitation (*upādhi*) of the one universal being.

The most important issue, however, for the School of Grammar comes in answer to the question, "What constitutes the meaning-unit of language?" It is here that the *Sphoṭa* theory is presented in direct challenge to all of the other positions reviewed above. In criticizing the *Mīmāṁsā*, *Vedānta* and *Nyāya* view that the individual letters or words of a sentence generate the meaning, the Grammarian points out that the letters of a word or the words in a sentence die away as soon as they are pronounced so that when we arrive at the last letter of a word or the last word of a sentence, the previous elements have all vanished. How then can the meaning of the whole word or sentence be cognized? If it is replied that memory holds the traces of the letters and words, this still does not help since, as only one thing can be cognized at a time in our mind, the memory traces will only replay the serial presentation of the original parts and no whole meaning will be generated. Therefore, says the Grammarian, since meaning is a single or unitary whole so also its generating condition must likewise be a whole. On this assumption the *Sphoṭa* theory is advanced—the idea that the word or sentence is an indivisible unity which is inherently given and engenders all meaning. The separate letters of a word or words of the sentence merely manifest the *Sphoṭa* or meaning-whole. In Mādhava's *Sarva-Darśana-Saṃgraha* the argument is put this way:

> ...as the letters cannot cause the cognition of the meaning, there must be a *sphoṭa* by means of which arises the knowledge of the meaning; and this *sphoṭa* is an eternal sound distinct

1. T.R.V. Murti, "Some Thoughts," pp. 14-15.

> from the letters and revealed by them, which causes the cognition of the meaning.[1]

In addition to such deductive argument, the Grammarians also appeal to common experience. The *sphoṭa* or unitary word-meaning, they argue, may be proved to exist in that it is an object of each person's own cognitive perception. When the word "go" ("cow") is pronounced there is the unitary perception or simultaneous cognition of dewlap, tail, hump, hoofs, horns, etc. in the hearer's mind. This perceivable *sphoṭa*, says the Grammarian, is exactly how Patañjali in his *Mahābhāṣya* defined "word" (taking "go" as his example) as that sound which when pronounced results in the simultaneous cognition of dewlap, tail, hump, hoofs, horns, etc. Verbal communication between people is only possible because of the existence of this *sphoṭa* or word-meaning which is potentially perceivable by all, and revealed to each individual by speech sounds.[2]

Although the conception of *sphoṭa*, and the arguments of this theory need to be examined in greater detail (see Part II), the above brief discussion suggests both a logical consistency in the Grammarian arguments and a persuasive appeal to our cognitive experience of whole meanings as grounds for selecting the *Sphoṭa* theory for serious study. Using Kantian thought as a model, Murti further describes the significance of the *Sphoṭa* conception as follows :

> In linguistic apprehension, as in other cognitions, there is the interplay of two factors of different levels—the empirical manifold of sense-data (the separate letters or words in this case) and the transcendental or *a priori* synthesis of the manifold which alone imparts a unity to those elements which would otherwise have remained a mere manifold.[3]

In this way of thinking the *sphoṭa* functions exactly like a transcendental category of the whole. It is through the *sphoṭa*, which is activated by the pronunciation or hearing of the separate letters or words, that the meaning of the sentence is manifested as a whole.

---

1. S. D., S. p. 211, Kunjunni Raja notes that *śabda* should be translated by "speech-unit" rather than "sound" (as Cowell does above) to avoid confusion between *śabda* and *dhvani*. Op. cit., p. 143.
2. *Ibid.*
3. T. R. V. Murti, "*Some Thoughts*," p. 17.

PART II

THE *SPHOṬA* THEORY OF LANGUAGE AS REVELATION

Now that its metaphysical background has been surveyed, I will proceed to analyze the logical[1] possibility of the *Sphoṭa* theory of language as revelation. Chapter Five begins with a definition of the concept of *sphoṭa* itself. In Chapter Six the way in which the *sphoṭa* reveals meaning is examined in detail with regard to both word-meaning and sentence-meaning. Chapter Seven studies *Sphoṭa* theory in relation to the various levels of language and meaning which are seen to result. Part II concludes with a summary of the major *sphoṭa* tenets, the logical[1] possibility of which has been demonstrated.

1. The reader is reminded that throughout this book the term "logical" is used not in a specialized philosophic sense, but as meaning "defensible on the grounds of consistency" or "reasonably to be believed."

Chapter Five

DEFINITION OF SPHOṬA

For the Grammarian, the word or sentence when taken as an indivisible meaning-unit is the *sphoṭa*. The technical term *sphoṭa* is difficult to translate into English. Sometimes the word "symbol" is used for *sphoṭa* in the sense of its function as a linguistic sign. One authority on the subject finds that the original Greek conception of *logos* best conveys the meaning of *sphoṭa*. G. Sastri argues, "The fact that *logos* stands for an idea as well as a word wonderfully approximates to the concept of *sphoṭa*."[1] The spoken sounds or printed letters of ordinary language are distinguished from the *sphoṭa* in that the former are merely the means by which the latter is revealed. The term *sphoṭa* is derived from the Sanskrit root *sphuṭ*, which means to burst forth. In his Sanskrit-English Dictionary, V. S. Apte defines *sphoṭa* as : (1) breaking forth, bursting or disclosure; and (2) the idea which bursts out or flashes on the mind when a sound is uttered.[2] In his *Sphoṭavāda*, Nāgeśa Bhaṭṭa describes *sphoṭa* in two ways : as that from which the meaning bursts or shines forth; and as an entity which is manifested by the spoken letters or sounds.[3] The *sphoṭa* may thus be thought of as a kind of two-sided coin. On the one side it is manifested by the word-sound, and on the other side it simultaneously reveals the word-meaning. In a more philosophic sense, *sphoṭa* may be described as the transcendent ground in which the spoken syllables and conveyed meaning find themselves united as word or *śabda*. Nāgeśa Bhaṭṭa identifies this theory with the teaching of the *ṛṣi* Sphoṭāyana, who the Grammarians claim to be the traditional formulator of their viewpoint. The original conception of *sphoṭa* seems to go far back into the Vedic period of Indian thought when, as was shown in the previous chapter, *vāk* or

1. Gaurinath Sastri, *The Philosophy of Word and Meaning*, pp. 102-103. Hereafter cited Sastri, *Word*.

2. V. S. Apte, *The Practical Sanskrit-English Dictionary*, p. 1013.

3. Nāgeśa Bhaṭṭa, *Sphoṭavāda*, p. 5.

speech was considered to be a manifestation of the all-pervading Brahman, and the *praṇava* (AUM) regarded as the primordial speech-sound from which all forms of *vāk* were supposed to have evolved. This sacred syllable is said to have flashed forth into the heart of *Brahman*, while he was absorbed in deep meditation, and to have given birth to the three *Vedas* containing all knowledge. AUM is still chanted today by devout Hindus who find the repetition of it to be at once a means of worship, knowledge, and a way of union with God (*mokṣa*). Our interest in the Vedic conception of the *praṇava* is that it seems to have provided the model upon which the later Grammarian philosophers based their conception of *sphoṭa*. In fact, *sphoṭa* is often identified with the *praṇava*. Chakravarti points out that the analogy between the two is so striking that Nāgeśa Bhaṭṭa does not hesitate to compare *sphoṭa* with the internal phase of *praṇava*.[1]

Although the Grammarians may have modelled their concept of *sphoṭa* on the Vedic *praṇava*, their method of approach was strikingly different. Rather than immersing themselves in mystical meditation, they set out to analyze the meanings of words and the means by which such word knowledge is manifested and communicated in ordinary experience. The Grammarian Patañjali provides the point of departure for such a study when he opens his *Mahābhāṣya* with the question, "What then is this word, 'cow'?", and answers "That—which when uttered, brings us knowledge of the object possessing dewlap, tail, hump, hooves and horns" is a word. He goes on to make clear that it is words spoken for communication purposes in popular language upon which he is focusing.[2] According to

1. P. C. Chakravarti, *The Philosophy of Sanskrit Grammar*, p. 89. Here after cited Chakravarti, *Philosophy*.

2. S. D. Joshi in a recent article argues that Patañjali is here really offering two different definitions of *śabda*. The second of these defines *śabda* as *dhvani*, thus allowing for the possibility of *śabda* as being a mere sound or noise which conveys no meaning. Since the *sphoṭa* is defined in terms of a meaning-unit-whole, says Joshi, this would only subsume the first alternative of Patañjali's definition. According to Joshi, the fact that the second alternative defines word in terms of sound only means that Patañjali remains open to the *Mīmāṁsaka* view that *śabda* is the sound (i.e., the aggregate of letters) even if it does not convey meaning. S. D. Joshi, "Patañjali's Definition of Word," in *Bulletin of the Deccan College Research Institute* 25, (1966), pp. 65-70.

Chakravarti, Patañjali recognized three prominent characteristics of *sphoṭa*, namely, unity, indivisibility, and eternity. With regard to the time required for the speaking of a word, Patañjali "observes that it is sound that seems to be either long or short, but what is manifested by sound, i.e. *sphoṭa*, is not at all affected by the variations of sound."[1] Thus, for Patañjali, *śabda* or word is seen as having the two aspects of *sphoṭa* and *dhvani* (sound), which are related as follows : *sphoṭa* represents what is *śabda* proper, whereas sound is only a quality serving to manifest the *sphoṭa*. When a word is spoken, variations such as speed of speaking, accent, etc., all occur at the level of the sound while the *sphoṭa* is held by Patañjali to remain unchanged.[2]

Chakravarti notes that on the basis of Patañjali's thought, *sphoṭa* though strictly one and indivisible, is also capable of being classified as internal and external. The internal form of *sphoṭa* is its innate expressiveness of the word-meaning. The external aspect of *sphoṭa* is the uttered sound (or written word) which is perceived by our sense organs but serves only to manifest or reveal the inner *sphoṭa* with its inherent word-meaning.[3] It is with Bhartṛhari, however, that these two aspects of *śabda* or *sphoṭa* are given systematic philosophical analysis. In his *Vākyapadīya*, Bhartṛhari states "In the words which are expressive the learned discern two aspects : the one [the *sphoṭa*] is the cause of the real word [while] the other [*dhvani*] is used to convey the meaning."[4] These two aspects, although they may appear to be essentially different, are really identical. The apparent difference is seen to result from the various external manifestations of the single internal *sphoṭa*. The process is explained as follows : At first the word exists in the mind of the speaker as a unity or *sphoṭa*. When he utters it, he produces a sequence of different sounds so that it appears to have differentiation. The listener, although first hearing a series of sounds, ultimately perceives the utterance as a unity—the same *sphoṭa* with which the speaker began—and it is then that the meaning is conveyed.[5]

---

1. Chakravarti, *Philosophy*, p. 99.
2. *Ibid.*
3. *Ibid.*, p. 100.
4. Vāk. I:44.
5. *Ibid.*, I:45-46.

In his discussion, Bhartṛhari employs several technical terms : *śabda/sphoṭa*, *dhvani*, and *nāda*. By *śabda* and/or *sphoṭa*, he refers to that inner unity which conveys the meaning. The *dhvanis* are described as all-pervasive and imperceptible particles which, when amassed by the movement of the articulatory organs, become gross and perceptible sounds and are then called *nāda*. These *nādas* function to suggest the word, *sphoṭa* or *śabda*. Since these *nādas*, which are gross and audible, have division and sequence, it is naturally assumed that the suggested word also has parts when in reality it is changeless and sequenceless.[1] Bhartṛhari offers the illustrative example of reflection in water. Just as an object reflected in water may seem to have movement because of the movement of the water, similarly the word or *sphoṭa* takes on the properties of uttered speech (e.g., sequence, loudness or softness, accent, etc.) in which it is manifested.[2]

Perhaps the reader can best understand Bhartṛhari's theory when it is illustrated with reference to our common experience of poetry. Let us take, for example, the word "love," which Bhartṛhari would call a *śabda* or *sphoṭa*. Although the meaning of the word love ultimately may be experienced as unitary, the communication of that insightful knowledge may well require the employment of a variety of suggestive poetic expressions :

Let me not to the marriage of true minds
Admit impediments. Love is not love
Which alters when it alteration finds,
Or bends with the remover to remove :
O, No ! it is an ever-fixed mark,
That looks on tempests, and is never shaken;
It is the star to every wandering bark,
Whose worth's unknown, although his height be taken.
Love's not Time's fool, though rosy lips and cheeks
Within his bending sickle's compass come;
Love alters not with his brief hours and weeks,
But bears it out even to the edge of doom.

1. Vāk. I:47.

2. *Ibid.*, I:49.

If this be error and upon me prov'd,
I never writ, nor no man ever lov'd.[1]

In this sonnet, Shakespeare, through the use of his poetic imagination, composes a variety of expressions which when uttered manifest in the listener's mind an intuitive perception of the word-symbol "love" and its meaning. Different people may experience the manifestation of unitary word-meaning differently. For some, it may come as a sudden flash of intuition, full-blown in its development. Others, however, may experience a gradual and progressive revelation through repeated exposures to the suggestive poetic phrases. In Bhartṛhari's theory, the word-*sphoṭa* "love" is a given, unitary and eternal in nature, but, as the history of literature, religion and marital relations evidences, it is a given requiring many gross *nādas* or imperfect empirical expressions before its meaning is fully grasped or intuitively realized in one's mind.

In Indian aesthetics, the philosophical analysis of language in terms of the *sphoṭa* theory seems to have been assumed as a basic premise.[2] The term *dhvani*, used in the *sphoṭa* theory, comes to occupy a central place in Indian aesthetics and receives further development in the hands of the literary critics. Whereas for the Grammarian *dhvani* referred to the imperceptible yet physical constituents of the gross utterances or *nādas*, the literary critics give the term *dhvani* a more specialized meaning. The utterance, "Love is unalterable, eternal, and matchless and ageless" would likely qualify, according to the Grammarians, as a *dhvani/nāda* sequence serving to manifest the word-*sphoṭa* "love." For Indian Aesthetics, however, something more is needed before such an external expression could be considered as a full revelation of the inner word-meaning, and therefore worthy of being called *dhvani*. That "something more" would be the kind of poetic expression encountered in Shakespeare's sonnet. The hallmark of such *dhvani* or greatness of poetic expression is that in it "the symbolic surpasses all the poetic elements in point of strikingness and shines in its full splendour

1. William Shakespeare, *The Works of William Shakespeare*. Sonnet 116, p. 1110.

2. For a convincing demonstration of this contention, see the recent study by Tarapada Chakrabarti, *Indian Aesthetics and Science of Language*. Hereafter cited Chakrabarti, *Aesthetics*.

as the cynosure of all minds."[1] Rather than just a dry philosophic making present of the word-meaning, the champion of Indian Aesthetics claims for *dhvani* a particular excellence in revelatory experience. According to Abhinavagupta, in the poetic experience of *dhvani* the transcendental function of suggestion removes the primordial veil of ignorance from our minds and thereby allows the bliss associated with the discovery of true meaning to be experienced. Such bliss is technically termed *rasa* and is held to be fully experienced when the poetic expression or *dhvani* removes the veil of ignorance so completely that the self of the experiencer stands clearly revealed. Abhinavagupta terms such an ultimate experience of *rasa* as "the delectable savouring of the self by the self."[2] The poet Hṛṣīkeśa defines *rasa* as "a fusion of both word and meaning [which] bathes the minds of sensitive readers with oozings of bliss. It is the truth of poetry, shining without cessation. Clear to the heart, it is yet beyond words."[3,4] It is probably true that the philosopher who painstakingly mines a particular concept so that its essential meaning stands clearly revealed also experiences a state of elation similar to that which the poet calls *rasa*. Although the Indian poet and the Grammarian philosopher might traverse somewhat different paths from the diversity of empirical expression to the realization of a unitary meaning, both seem to agree that in the end a common goal is achieved—

1. Chakrabarti, *Aesthetics*, p. 146.
2. *Ibid.*, p. 143.
3. As quoted in J. L. Mason and M. V. Patwardhan, *Aesthetic Rapture: The Rasādhyāya of the Nāṭyaśāstra*, p. 26.
4. In his critical analysis of the *rasa* concept, V. K. Chari defends it from the Western criticism of subjectivism or mysticism as follows : "This objection may be answered by saying that if the Rasa theorists emphasize the essential privacy of the aesthetic experience—and it must be admitted that they do so rightly enough for Rasa, being but a datum of our consciousness, cannot be verified by empirical means—they also assume that it has its foundation in universal human nature. And in this sense, it is not so much subjective as inter-subjective. Without assuming such an affinity of nature between the poet and the reader on the one hand, and between a community of readers on the other, no aesthetic communication would be conceivable." See '*Rasa*' *As An Aesthetic Concept* : *Some Comments from the Point of View of Western Criticism*. Unpublished paper presented by V. K. Chari at the "International Sanskrit Conference," New Delhi, March 31st, (1972), p. 7. This seems similar to Kant's understanding of the universal but subjective nature of aesthetic judgment as outlined in his *Critique of Judgment*.

the joyful revelation of the word-*sphoṭa* as envisaged by Bhartṛhari.[1]

Having described the *sphoṭa* concept, let us now briefly restate its definition in a simple diagram :

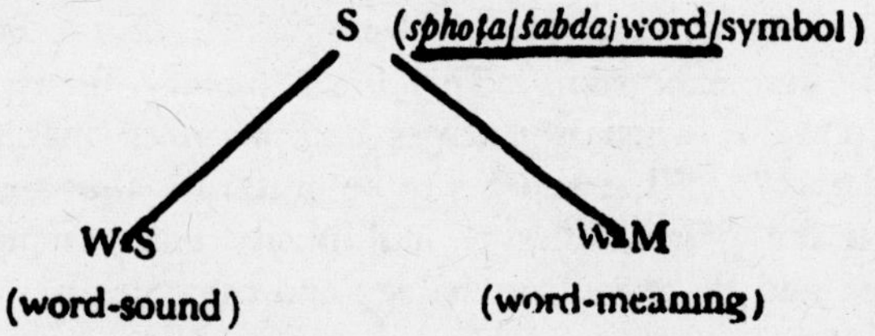

It must be emphasized that, according to Bhartṛhari, the *sphoṭa* is an indivisible and changeless unity. But in terms of its communication or revelation function, it may be heuristically represented (in the above diagram) as having two aspects. It is like a two-sided coin. Its external aspect is the uttered sound or written word which is perceived by our sense organs but serves only to manifest the *sphoṭa's* inner aspect. The inner aspect is the expressive word-meaning which inherently resides in all beings. When a person wants to communicate an idea or word-meaning, he begins with the *sphoṭa* which has been inherently existing in his mind as a unity. When he utters it and produces different sounds in sequence by the movements of his articulatory organs, it appears to have differentiation. But the listener, as he hears the sound sequence, ultimately perceives it as a unity (*sphoṭa*), and only then is the word-meaning, which is also inherently present in the listener's mind, identified or revealed.[2] The question as to just how such a communication of word-*sphoṭas* can occur will be examined in the next section of this chapter. The point of focus in this definition is simply the Grammarians' contention that the basic unit of language is the given whole (the *sphoṭa* subsuming both the word-sound and the word-meaning) and the summed sequence of spoken sounds or written letters.

---

1. See Chakrabarti, *Aesthetics*, pp. 146-149.

2. The above diagram is a modified version of the one presented by D. M. Datta, in *The Six Ways of Knowing*, p. 257.

Reason for the Phenomenalization of the Sphoṭa

If it is assumed with the Grammarians that the whole or *sphoṭa* is the basic unit of language, the question may then arise as to why this unity should ever come to be expressed in the phenomenal diversity which is commonly called speech. In Bhartṛhari's view, such phenomenalization occurs because the *sphoṭa* itself contains an inner energy (*kratu*) which seeks to burst forth (*sphuṭ*) into expression. This inner latency Bhartṛhari calls *śakti* (power); when it emerges and becomes manifest, it is termed *vyakti*. What appears to be unitary is thus seen to contain all the potentialities of multiplicity and complexity like the seed and the sprout or the egg and the chicken.

> The external (audible) word, employed in verbal usage is merged in the mind after suppressing all assumption of differentiation, without, however, abandoning the residual force of the differentiation, as in the case of the yolk in the egg of the pea-hen. Just as one single word can merge, so can passages consisting of as many as ten parts. The word, thus merged, with all differentiation suppressed, again assumes differentiation and sequence, when through the speaker's desire to say something, the inner word is awakened and it becomes the sentence or the word, each with its divisions.[1]

Here Bhartṛhari seems to be suggesting two ways in which the energy of speech (*kratu*) causes the phenomenalization of the *sphoṭa*. On the one hand, there is the pent-up potentiality for bursting forth residing in the *sphoṭa* itself, while on the other hand there is the desire of the speaker to communicate. This desire for communication, however, is described as existing solely for the purpose of revealing the *sphoṭa* that is within.[2] Unlike thinkers who conceive of language in conventional or utilitarian terms,[3] Bhartṛhari finds language to contain and reveal its own *telos*. In his metaphysical speculations, with which we are not primarily concerned, Bhartṛhari identifies this *telos* with

1. Vāk., *Vṛtti* on I:51, p. 58.
2. *Ibid.*, I:1 *Vṛtti*, p. 1.
3. For example, the early Buddhists, the *Cārvākas*, or in modern thought the Positivists.

Brahman who is beginningless and endless and whose essence is the word (*śabdatattva*). Bhartṛhari, in fact, takes his position to the logical extreme and concludes, in line with the Vedic Seers, that from speech (*vāk*) the creation of the whole world proceeds.

At this point the question might well be raised as to how the Grammarian view of the phenomenalization of the absolute compares with the *Advaita Vedānta* theory. On the surface there are apparent parallels. For both the Vedāntin and the Grammarian the world of phenomenal differentiation appears as a free act of the absolute, yet the absolute is judged to be in no way diminished by the phenomenalization But, from Bhartṛhari's viewpoint, is this phenomenalization a case of *vivarta* (an unreal appearance) in the Vedāntin sense, or is it a *pariṇāma* (a real transformation) in the Sāṅkhyan sense, or is it something else ? As yet, there seems no definitive answer to this question. In recent years, two scholars[1] have given this issue serious study, each coming to different conclusions. Their findings are briefly summarized as follows :

G. Sastri points out that at the time of Bhartṛhari terms such as *pariṇāma* and *vivarta* did not likely possess the fine philosophical distinctions which they later were given—especially in the hands of Śaṅkara and his followers. In the hands of Bhartṛhari, says Sastri, the status of the phenomenal words in relation to *Śabda-brahman* cannot be adequately characterized by either *pariṇāma* or *vivarta* in their respective doctrinal formulations. Bhartṛhari does not believe in any real change of *Śabdabrahman*; therefore, the Sāṅkhyan conception of *pariṇāma* is ruled out. Nor does the *Vākyapadīya* seem to contain exactly the same kind of logical antinomy between the ground (as an indivisible unity) and its appearances that led Śaṅkara to invoke the *vivarta* concept. According to Sastri's reading, Bhartṛhari does not conceive of any difference between *Śabdabrahman* and its *śaktis* (powers or appearances)—the being (*Śabdabrahman*) and its powers (*śaktis*) are identical. Thus since Bhartṛhari sees no difference to be accounted for, the concept of *vivarta* (with its intent of accounting for the difference between the diversity of phenomena in relation to the unitary absolute) does not really

1. They are Gaurinath Sastri and K. A. S. Iyer. The following summary is based on Sastri, *Word*, pp. 45-65, and K. A. Subramania Iyer, *Bhartṛhari*, pp. 128-135. See also "Some Thoughts," p. 15.

apply. Instead of either the *pariṇāma* or the *vivarta* doctrinal viewpoints, Sastri suggests the Bhartṛhari's position is much closer to the notion of "reflection" (*ābhāsa*) formulated by the Trika writers of Kashmir. In this view the *śaktis* and their phenomenal manifestation as words are identical with the Absolute. The relationship between the two described on the analogy of the mirror (the absolute) and its reflections (the *ābhāsas*); the latter can have no independent existence without the former—yet, the latter also have a reality which is somehow identical with the former. Sastri maintains that the many of Bhartṛhari's commentators have failed to realize the above distinctions because they have read the *Vākyapadiya* under the influence of later Vedāntic *vivarta* formulations.

Iyer, however, claims strong evidence for interpreting Bhartṛhari's thought in line with traditional *Vedānta* doctrine. Iyer bases his interpretation on the assumption that Bhartṛhari is the author of the *Vṛtti* (as tradition maintains), although he admits that this question is not yet finally settled. Iyer documents how, according to Bhartṛhari, in ordinary life we can neither cognize nor express the absolute directly in words. There is, however, something which runs through these unreal word forms (*asatyopādhi*) and which persists when such forms disappear. That is, *Brahman*, the ultimate reality, and the expressed meaning of all words. Bhartṛhari seems to offer two different ways of interpreting this situation. One viewpoint, associated with Vājapyāyana, holds that the persisting aspect of the word is the universal (*jāti*) which it connotes. Although in ordinary language we may validly speak of several universals such as man, cow, horse, etc., there is only one ultimate universal being, and all phenomenal word-forms mean this. The other interpretation, attributed to Vyāḍi, suggests that being or substance is that which persists and is perceived as the individual (*dravya*) through a limitation (*upādhi*) of that universal being. Word-meaning in this view is the denotation or the "that" of things. Ultimately there is only the one indivisible *Brahman*, which is the meaning of all limiting individual word-forms. Men, cows, horses, etc. are merely appearances through the limitation of that Being. Such limitations are described by Bhartṛhari as *asatya* (false or unreal). It is these unreal limiting factors which words first denote before pointing beyond themselves to the ultimate reality. The real is thus cognized only through the unreal word-forms. Both of these viewpoints would be consistent with a *vivarta* interpretation.

Bhartṛhari himself, claims Iyer, seems to admit the parallelism between his position and that of *Vedānta* for he openly refers to the followers of *Trayyanta* (i.e., *Vedānta*), and seems to consider himself to be one of them. His repeated description of the cognized phenomenal world as "*asatya*" and his declaration that "*satya*" is that which, although free from all differentiation, assumes differentiation, is cited by Iyer as strong evidence for attributing to Bhartṛhari a *vivarta* theory very close to that of *Advaita Vedānta*. This is further supported by Bhartṛhari's repeated reference to *avidyā* as the cosmic power by which the one changeless reality is presented as having many word-forms arranged in a spatial and temporal sequence. Helārāja, commenting on the *Vṛtti*, maintains that the undifferentiated ultimate reality becomes differentiated and assumes an infinite number of forms due to the beginningless influence of *avidyā*. Although he notes that the two words *pariṇāma* and *vyavarta* appear more or less as synonyms in *Vākyapadīya* I:112 in the description of the emergence of the phenomenal world from the *Śabdabrahman*, Iyer concludes that all the available ancient commentaries, beginning with the *Vṛtti*, interpret Bhartṛhari's thought as *vivartavāda*.

In concluding this observation on the apparent parallel between Bhartṛhari and *Advaita Vedānta*, it is again noted that as yet there seems to be no definite answer to this question. That further research is required becomes even more evident when (as is observed later in Chapter Six) Bhartṛhari's treatment of error as a case of progressive perceptual approximation to the real is compared with the *Advaita* view in which there can be only "true" or "false" cognitions with no gradations in between.

Returning to Bhartṛhari's assumption that from *Śabdabrahman* the creation of the whole world proceeds, the following logical deduction is seen to result. "There is no cognition without the operation of the word/*sphoṭa*."[1] This seems to agree with the

1. Vāk. I:123. Related to this point is the Grammarian's rejection of gestures as vehicles for communicating meaning. As Puṇyarāja puts it, the shaking of the head indicating negation does not communicate independent of words. The gesture serves to make one think of the word "no" before it can communicate the meaning of negation or refusal. See P. K. Chakravarti, *The Linguistic Speculations of the Hindus*, p. 72. Hereafter cited Chakravarti, *Linguistic*.

contention of at least one modern linguist that there is no thought without language.[1] As Professor T. R. V. Murti puts it, it is not that we have a thought and then look for a word with which to express it; or that we have a lonely word which we seek to connect with a thought. "Word and thought develop together, or rather they are the expressions of one deep spiritual impulse to know and to communicate."[2]

Sphoṭa Defined as Sentence (*Vākya-Sphoṭa*)

In the above it has been made clear that Bhartṛhari conceives of all beings as born with *śabda* or speech already present within. Metaphysically he identifies it with the self (*ātman*). Already at birth the new-born child has it, although as yet he knows no language in the ordinary sense of the word. As the child grows this inner *śabda*, which potentially can be developed into any language, is transformed into the language of the particular speech-community into which the child was born. Although little is known about how such transformation takes place, Bhartṛhari makes certain basic assumptions in regard to the process. The first is that *śabda* or the word as it exists in the consciousness of even the new-born baby has the dual aspects of the word-meaning or the expressive aspect (*vācaka*) and the word-sound or the expressed element (*vācya*). This was illustrated in the above diagram. This differentiation of the ultimately unitary *śabda* (*śabdatattva*) into its two aspects is said to take place as soon as the metaphysical word-principle takes the form of mind (*manas*) or intellect (*buddhi*), and is technically referred to as "the *buddhi* stage."[3] The concern of this book is not directed to the metaphysical speculations regarding the ultimate nature of *śabda*, but rather focuses upon the question as to how *śabda* in the *buddhi* stage (and below) both conveys and reveals meaning. Therefore, it is the second major assumption for Bhartṛhari which is perhaps of greater interest for our present purpose. That is, the assumption that the whole is primary and its differentiated parts are secondary. For Bhartṛhari, it is the whole idea or complete thought which is the *vācaka*—

1. See Edward Sapir, *Language*, p. 15.
2. T. R. V. Murti, "Some Thoughts," p. iii.
3. See Iyer, *Bhartṛhari*, p. 151.

the word-meaning or expressive aspect of *śabda* as *sphoṭa*. When the young child utters his first single word ejaculations, "mama," "dog", "cookie," etc., it is clear that whole ideas (as yet incompletely expressed) are being verbalized : e.g., "I want mama !," "See the dog," "Give me a cookie !", etc. Even when a word is used merely in the form of a substantive noun (e.g., "tree"), the verb "to be" is always understood so that what is indicated is really a complete thought (e.g., "It is a tree").[1]

Bhartṛhari opposes the views of other Schools such as the *Mīmāṁsakas* and *Nyāya-Vaiśeṣikas*, who claim that the young child learns language by observing the use of words by grown-ups until the meaning of each individual word is understood. These philosophers conceive the sentence meaning or the complete thought as resulting from the summation of the individual word meanings. Bhartṛhari observes, however, that man does not speak in individual words. For him the chief reality in linguistic communication is the idea or meaning-whole of the indivisible sentence. Although he sometimes speaks about letters (*varṇa*) or individual words (*pada*) as meaning-bearing units (*sphoṭa*), it is clear that for Bhartṛhari the true form of the *sphoṭa* is the sentence.[2] K. A. Subramania Iyer clearly summarizes Bhartṛhari's position :

> What Bhartṛhari tries to establish is that the sentence and the sentence-meaning are indivisible units and that they alone are real (*satya*). Individual words and their meanings have neither definiteness nor reality. Communication is done with sentences and not with individual words. Communication means the transference of what the speaker has in mind to his hearer. What he has in mind may be a fact or a fantasy, but it exists as a unity and the word through which he communicates it also exists as a unity. This unity is the sentence. When the hearer also grasps this unity, both of the word and of the meaning, communication has taken place.[3]

1. See Vāk., *Vṛtti* on I:24-26, p. 31.
2. *Ibid.*, see especially the *Second Kāṇḍa* in which he establishes the *vākya-sphoṭa* over against the view of the *Mīmāṁsakas*.
3. Iyer, *Bhartṛhari*, p. 182.

The listener grasps the unity of meaning conveyed by the words of the sentence in a flash of insight or intuition which Bhartṛhari technically terms *pratibhā*.[1] *Pratibhā*, in Indian thought, is described as a super-normal perception which transcends the ordinary categories of time, space and causality, and has the capacity to directly "grasp" the real nature of things. Such super-normal perceptions are held to perceive the object in its noumenal wholeness, and to have totally transcended phenomenal characteristics such as name and form. Consequently, *pratibhā* cannot be understood by appealing to the phenomenal facts of ordinary perceptions. Aside from one's personal experience of such super-normal perception, there can only be speculative attempts at description which, because they are on the phenomenal level of name and form, will always fall short. The *pratibhā* experience is that of a unified psychic entity. It is in this sense that Bhartṛhari connects *pratibhā* with the *vākya-sphoṭa*. The sentence is really a psychic entity, a mental symbol which in itself is the meaning. The mental perception of this *vākya-sphoṭa* is a case of *pratibhā*. Although it is quite different from the meanings of the individual words, it is through the meanings of the individual words that the *pratibhā* of the *vākya-sphoṭa* occurs. Because the whole sentence meaning is inherently present in the mind of each person, it is quite possible for the *pratibhā* of the *sphoṭa* to be grasped by the listener even before the whole sentence has been uttered. More often, however, inference and reasoning may have to be applied to the words of the sentence so that the individual's cognition is brought to the level where the intuitive grasping (*pratibhā*) of the meaning whole (*vākya-sphoṭa*) becomes possible. It is in this sense that reason is taken as the precursor of the revelatory experience.

Bhartṛhari also uses the term *pratibhā* as a broad general concept which is realizable in six different ways ranging all the way from the instinctive knowledge of animals to the perfect perception or special intuition of the *ṛṣis* (*viśiṣṭopahita*). A more detailed discussion of *pratibhā* is undertaken later in Chapter Six.

1. See K. R. Pillai, The *Vākyapadīya*, II:153 ff, pp. 72-73.

Variations in the Definitions of Sphoṭa

Although Bhartṛhari's conception of *sphoṭa* as outlined above, is undoubtedly the dominant view for the Grammarian School,[1] there was evidently some difference of opinion among the ancient Indian grammarians as to the real nature of the *sphoṭa*. Bhartṛhari mentions some of these definitions of *sphoṭa* which differ from his own.

According to one of these variant views, the initial sounds produced by the contacts and separations of the vocal organs are themselves the *sphoṭas*, and not the mere manifestors of the *sphoṭas* as Bhartṛhari maintains.[2] As these initial sounds are momentary, the *sphoṭas* are also held to be momentary. The sound waves resulting from the initial sound produced by the vocal organs, and which spread in all directions decreasing in strength until reaching the ears of the hearers, are called the *dhvanis*. These *dhvanis* are said to have the nature of reverberation. This reverberation is thought of as a chain of repetitions of the initial sound or *sphoṭa*. Each link in this chain of rever berations is weaker than the preceding one, but is still in reflection of the initial *sphoṭa*. Just as the reverberation of a drum lasts longer and reaches further than the noise of a piece of metal, so it is the nature of the initial sound or *sphoṭa* which is instrumental in producing a reverberation chain of shorter or longer duration. In this view both the *dhvani* reverberations and the initial *sphoṭa* sounds are held to be momentary.[3]

Another theory differing only slightly from the previous one holds that the *sphoṭa* and the *dhvanis* are produced simultaneously.[4] Whereas in the above view the *sphoṭa* is produced prior to the *dhvanis*, here there is no interval between the production of the *sphoṭa* and the *dhvanis*. The *sphoṭa* is described as the material cause of the sound and is compared to a flame; t *dhvanis* are like the light spreading in all directions.[5] Iyer observes that here also the *sphoṭa* is held to be transitory, and that

1. Evidence for this is that it is Bhartṛhari's conception of *sphoṭa* that the opposing schools of philosophy cite as the *Sphoṭa* Theory or the Grammarian viewpoint : e.g., Kumārila's *Ślokavārttika*, *sūtra* V, section 12; and Ś. B. B. S. I:3:28.

2. See Vāk. I:102, p. 97.

3. *Ibid.*, *Vṛtti* on I:102.

4. *Ibid.*, I:104, p. 99.

5. See Raja, *Theories*, p. 114.

this view is put forward to answer a possible objection that the sound, apart from the *sphoṭa* does not exist at all. It is argued that both *dhvanis* and *sphoṭa* exist separately even though they may not always be perceived as such. Sometimes, for example, we may hear the *dhvanis* (e.g., crowd noises) without recognizing or distinguishing the actual *sphoṭas* (e.g., the words being spoken). Both co-exist, however, and are being produced simultaneously.[1]

In contrast to the two above variant views which define *sphoṭa* as ephemeral and produced by human effort, Bhartṛhari reports yet another theory. This theory is closer to Bhartṛhari's own position in that it views the *sphoṭa* as the changeless word which is caused by the different sounds or *dhvanis*.[2] Iyer states, "The main idea here is that the sounds, which differ from one another because of difference in articulatory movements, cause the cognition of the one changeless word without effecting any change in it, just as the light from a lamp reveals the object without effecting any change in it."[3] The *Vṛtti* makes clear that the *sphoṭa* here is being viewed as the universal and the *dhvanis* as the class members. Kunjunni Raja makes a helpful observation in this regard.

> Many scholars have taken this theory as that of Bhartṛhari himself... Here it is important to note that for Bhartṛhari the *sphoṭa* is the word or the sentence taken as a single meaningful unit; if he accepts the concept of a class, it will be a class whose members are themselves *sphoṭas*. The identification of *sphoṭa* with the class of *dhvanis*, without any reference to the meaning-bearing aspect, is entirely against Bhartṛhari's conception of *sphoṭa*.[4]

Having taken note of these variant views mentioned by Bhartṛhari, let us clearly restate his own definition of *sphoṭa*. For Bhartṛhari, the two aspects of word-sound (*dhvani*) and word-meaning (*artha*), differentiated in the mind and yet integrated like two sides of the same coin, constitute the *sphoṭa*.[5] He

1. See Vāk., Translator's note on I:104, p. 100.
2. *Ibid.*, I:94, p. 92.
3. *Ibid.*, note 1 to I:94, p. 92.
4. Raja, *Theories*, p. 115.
5. This and the following statements are based upon Iyer's excellent summary of Bhartṛhari's definition of *sphoṭa*, in *Bhartṛhari*, pp. 177-180.

emphasizes the meaning-bearing or revelatory function of this two-sided unity, the *sphoṭa*, which he maintains is eternal and given in nature. He generally describes one's cognition of the *sphoṭa* from the hearer's perspective. As a child learning a word, or as an adult on first hearing a word, the *sphoṭa* is usually at first cognized erroneously. Having failed to grasp the whole *sphoṭa* the listener asks, "What did you say?" Through a series of erroneous cognitions, in response to the repeated vocalizations of the word-sounds, there arises a progressively clearer cognition of the *sphoṭa*. Finally there is a completely clear cognition of the whole *sphoṭa* and its two-sided aspects which Bhartṛhari describes as a case of special perception, intuition or *pratibhā*. The initial error has given place to truth in which the two aspects of word-sound and word-meaning have become completely identical in the unity of the *sphoṭa*. Since the cognition of this final and *a priori sphoṭa* unity is held to be a case of perception (*pratibhā*), various perceptual analogies are offered as examples. When from a distance a tree is vaguely cognized, the cognition may take the form of an elephant. When finally, through repeated effort, it is recognized as a tree, the cognition is clearly a case of perception. Or when the expert jeweller finally sees the genuineness of a precious stone after a continuous gaze at it consisting of a series of comparatively vague cognitions of it, it is a case of perception. Bhartṛhari claims that means of knowledge other than perception (e.g., inference) either reveal the object or do not reveal it at all. It is only perception where the object (in this case the word-meaning) is at first seen vaguely and then more and more clearly. While all of this is the process experienced by ordinary men, Bhartṛhari, along with most other Indian Philosophers, allows that the great *ṛṣis* are able to cognize the complete unitary *sphoṭa* directly, without having to go through the process of repeated perception and error correction. In the previous Chapter, this *viśiṣṭopahita pratibhā* exhibited by the *ṛṣi* was referred to as his *dhī* or clear vision of reality, which he verbalized in the poetic form of the *Vedas*.[1]

---

1. It should perhaps be noted here that just as *pratibhā* (realizable through six ways) is inherent in all beings, so too *Veda* and *Āgama*, the real counterpart of *pratibhā*, exists within everyone. See Iyer, *Bhartṛhari*, pp. 90-91.

In concluding this discussion, let us make one observation regarding Bhartṛhari's definition of *sphoṭa*. Such direct perception of reality, described above as characteristic of the *ṛṣi*, does not properly fall within the scope of Bhartṛhari's definition of *sphoṭa*. Describing the process of the *sphoṭa's* manifestation in ordinary communication, Bhartṛhari emphasizes that when manifested by the sounds it is grasped by the mind—making clear it is only in the *buddhi* stage where the two aspects appear differentiated that the term *sphoṭa* can be applied. In the pre-*buddhi* stage (the level at which the *ṛṣi* functions), there is no separation into the two aspects of word-sound and word-meaning, and the technical term used here is *śabdatattva* rather than *sphoṭa*.[1]

1. See Iyer, *Bhartṛhari*, p. 180.

Chapter Six

HOW THE SPHOṬA REVEALS MEANING

Introduction

The Grammarian *Sphoṭa* Theory as officially expounded by Bhartṛhari attracted both opponents and supporters. The chief opposition came, at a later time, from the *Mīmāṁsaka* Kumārila Bhaṭṭa. Kumārila's attack focused on the way in which the *Sphoṭa* theory conceived of word-sounds as revealing their meanings. The side of Bhartṛhari in this debate against Kumārila was taken by the skilful philosopher Maṇḍana Miśra. Maṇḍana's work entitled *Sphoṭasiddhi*, which is based on the *Vākyapadiya*, records the confrontation that takes place on this issue of how the word conveys meaning, and it will be the main source for the section on *sphoṭa* and word-meaning. For Bhartṛhari, with his assumption of the whole as being prior to the parts, it is not the individual words but the complete thought of the sentence that ultimately matters. This will be examined under the heading "*Sphoṭa* and Sentence-Meaning."

Sphoṭa and Word-Meaning (pada-sphoṭa)

In the above definition of *sphoṭa* (Chapter Five) we have seen how Bhartṛhari maintains that the external word-sound should not be taken as the objective reality since it serves only to reveal the inner word-meaning which is both a unified whole and the true object. Illustrations, such as the poetic experience, have been offered to support Bhartṛhari's view that it is the whole word or idea which occasions sound and not vice versa. While such illustrations from ordinary experience can indicate that the *Sphoṭa* theory is not implausible, they can hardly be taken as proof of the theory's logical possibility. The latter requires that the existence of the inner word, as distinct from its sounds, be demonstrated in terms of logical necessity and consistency. This is precisely the task undertaken by Maṇḍana Miśra in his *Sphoṭasiddhi*.[1] Maṇḍana applies his logical analysis not only

1. See K. A. Subramania Iyer, trans., *Sphoṭasiddhi of Maṇḍana Miśra*. All quotations from the *Sphoṭasiddhi* are taken from this translation. Hereafter cited Iyer, *Sphoṭasiddhi*.

to the *Sphoṭa* theory but also to the alternative hypothesis put forth by Kumārila.[1] As Gaurinath Sastri observes, Kumārila was the most formidable critic of the *Sphoṭa* theory—later writers have offered no new criticisms but only repeat Kumārila's arguments.[2] Kumārila, arguing against Bhartṛhari, maintains that the word or *śabda*, whether it be the sentence or the individual word, is nothing more than a collection of word-sounds or spoken letters, and it is with this collection alone that the word-meaning is associated. When such a collection is brought to the mind of the hearer by the sounds uttered by the speaker, the hearer understands the meaning from the sounds alone. No mystical entity, such as *sphoṭa*, need be postulated at all.[3] According to Bhartṛhari, however, "the essence of the *Sphoṭa* doctrine is the idea that the word, mainly in the form of the sentence and secondarily in the form of the individual word and the phoneme [the articulated letter sound], is the entity over and above the sounds and not a mere collection of them and that it is this entity which is the bearer of the meaning."[4] This is the argument in its most general form. Let us now analyze it in detail.

The discussion begins with a statement of Patañjali's famous question, "What is meant by 'word'?" and his answer, "Speech or *śabda*."[5] Here Patañjali is defining *śabda* as that which has a meaning. Kumārila objects by noting that in the first place a definition in terms of meaning alone is too wide. Smoke, for example, signifies the meaning fire, but is not commonly regarded as a word for fire. In the second place, says Kumārila, the definition is too narrow in that it holds *śabda* to be that which is heard. Now, that which is perceived by the ear is only a group of phonemes or letter-sounds, each one of which (according to Patañjali's definition) should be regarded as a word even though they do not signify any external fact. This results in the difficulty that in the word "cow," for example, the individual phonemes "c," "o," and "w" may be heard by

1. The context and basis of Kumārila's argument was noted in Chapter Two in the summary of the *Mīmāṁsaka* viewpoint.

2. See Sastri, *Word*, p. 103.

3. See Jha, *Ślokavārttika*, *sūtra* V, Section 12, pp. 261-268.

4. See Iyer, *Sphoṭasiddhi*, "Introduction," p. 3.

5. See Sph., *Kārikā* 3, p. 2.

the ear of the young child, and therefore qualify as *śabda* even though the word "cow" as yet carries no meaning for him. This clearly conflicts with Patañjali's contention that *śabda* is that significant word-whole which conveys meaning. Consequently, the spoken word "cow" would at the same time be *śabda* and not-*śabda*. It would be *śabda* in the sense that it consists in a commonly understood spoken word, but it would not be *śabda* before its meaning was known—although it would become *śabda* after its meaning is known. For these three reasons : (1) that smoke should not be called *śabda* even though it causes the cognition of fire, (2) that phonemes, even though they are audible, should not be called *śabda*, and (3) that the same thing should at one moment be called *aśabda* and the next moment *śabda*, Kumārila says that Patañjali's definition of *śabda* as interpreted by the Grammarians is not correct.[1] In Kumārila's view, it is the fact of being audible which should be taken as the criterion for *śabda*, and it is the phonemes alone (even though they may not convey meaning) which conform to this standard.[2] It is the phonemes which are commonly accepted as *śabda*. Anything which is different from the phonemes, or over and above them (e.g., *sphoṭa*—even though it may have existence and expressive power), does not deserve to be called *śabda* since there is no such common usage in the world.

Maṇḍana rejects Kumārila's criticism as frivolous misinterpretation. Saying that the signifying power is the criterion condition for *śabda* does not mean that a word ceases to be a word when it fails to communicate a meaning to an unlearned child or a dunce. According to the Grammarian, the key point is that the word is capable of conveying meaning—regardless of its being understood or not understood in specific instances. And since the phonemes or letters which constitute a word do not have this capacity individually, they cannot be called *śabda*. Having refuted Kumārila in this summary fashion, Maṇḍana goes on to elucidate the Grammarian interpretation of "*śabda*" in answer to Patañjali's question : "In that complex cognition expressed by the word 'cow' and which consists of many aspects

1. See Sph., *Kārikā* 3, p. 3.

2. This statement is made at this point only for the sake of argument, since Kumārila actually believes that it is the phonemes which convey the meaning. *Ibid.*, note 3.

such as the universal, the particular, quality, action, phonemes, *sphoṭa*, etc., which aspect is it to which the name *śabda* refers ?"[1] *Śabda*, maintains Maṇḍana, cannot refer to the individual phonemes because in themselves they convey no meaning. In common experience the whole word is the unit of language which is taken to be meaning-bearing. The common man takes a noun or verb to be a unity signifying meaning—without reference to the plurality of letters and syllables which are the products of speculative thought. Maṇḍana further criticizes Kumārila's objections and establishes the basis for the *Sphoṭa* position as follows :

> As for the definition that a word is what is cognized by the auditory sense-organ, it is vitiated by serious defects. The auditory organ also apprehends qualitative differences of pitch and modulation and such universals as wordhood and the like. These attributes though known through the organ of hearing are not words. Moreover, word is not known only by the auditory organ but also by the mind. So the definition proposed by Kumārila is misleading and apt to create confusion. The verdict of unsophisticated common sense that 'cow' is a whole word which yields meaning, ought not to be brushed aside as an uncritical appraisal. The unity of the significant word is a felt fact and no amount of quibbling can conjure it away.[2]

Of the various aspects of the complex cognition "cow," Maṇḍana makes clear that it is the *sphoṭa* or felt word-unity which is capable of conveying meaning and therefore is the essential characteristic—without which it would cease to be what it is (*lakṣaṇa*). Other aspects of the complex cognition such as the particular, the quality, the phonemes, etc., are merely occasional aspects (as in the usual example of a crow sitting on a house) and therefore are called *upalakṣaṇa*.

The next stop in the argument occurs when Kumārila extends his definition of the phonemes as *śabda* to rest not only on their

1. K. A. Subramania Iyer, "The Doctrine of Sphoṭa," in *Journal of the Ganganatha Jha Research Institute*, vol. 5, p. 124. Hereafter cited Iyer, "Doctrine."

2. A summary of part of Maṇḍana's answer to Kumārila, *Sphoṭasiddhi*, *Kārikā* 3 (cd) as presented by G. Sastri, *Word*, p. 105.

uttered quality but also now on the contention that it is they (and not a so-called *sphoṭa*) that cause the understanding of meaning. "Why not say that the phonemes themselves are the cause of the understanding of meaning and that, when grouped according to units of meaning which are understood, they are called words (*pada*) ?"[1]

In rebutting this new contention that it is the phonemes which convey meaning, Maṇḍana reasons as follows. Phonemes cannot singly convey the meaning since, as Kumārila admits, a collection of them in the form of a word or *pada* is needed. Nor can the phonemes co-exist as a *pada* since they are uttered singly and perceived in a certain order. When they are spoken by different speakers or in a different order or at the same time they do not convey a meaning. At no time can all the phonemes or letters of a word exist together and work together; their individual natures, being eternal and unchanging, are such that no joint simultaneity is possible. Phonemes are necessarily successive and therefore cannot work together to produce a *pada* which conveys a meaning. Therefore, the understanding of meaning which cannot be due to the phonemes points to a cause which is something different from the phonemes (*varṇas*).[2]

Kumārila counters this rebuttal by giving further development to the *Mīmāṁsaka* view as stated in the *Śabara Bhāṣya* on *Mīmāṁsā* Sūtra 1.1.5. Let it be admitted that the understanding of meaning does not take place from the phonemes in their individual condition, but if when grouped as *pada* they are seen to acquire some special efficacy which provides for the conveying of meaning. What then remains to block the acceptance of the collection of phonemes alone as *pada*? Nothing is required but the phonemes. Without them, however, there is no possibility of conveying meaning. In this regard, the case of the phoneme is very much like that of the common seed. The seed will not produce a new effect (a sprout) as long as it is isolated, but when it is helped by a group of other factors such as soil, moisture, etc., the sprout appears. Now the sprout is commonly judged as being the effect of the seen when combined with a group of helping factors. Similarly, these phonemes

1. Sph.. *Kārikā* 4. p. 10.
2. *Ibid.*

when combined with a group of helping factors (such as being uttered by the same person in a particular sequence) are commonly held to become the cause of the understanding of meaning. As a parting shot, Kumārila invokes a principle of "economy" : "As long as there is a visible cause and a visible mode of its being, there is no occasion for thinking of an invisible cause."[1]

In reply to this, Maṇḍana admits that a special efficacy may be shown to be the property of an otherwise ordinary cause, but maintains that it is just that special efficacy which has not been demonstrated in the case of phonemes as potential conveyers of meaning. Maṇḍana asks, what is the difference between "o" in the word "go" (cow) and an isolated "o" ? The obvious difference is that in one instance the "o" is isolated while in the word it is accompanied by another phoneme. But can this really be called accompaniment when, by the time of the speaking or hearing of the "o," the other phoneme is no longer being perceived at all ? A previously uttered phoneme, which has ceased to exist leaving no trace, and an unborn phoneme (or one which is as yet unspoken) are on the same footing. If previously spoken phonemes can be said to give help to a successor, then it should also be admitted that unspoken phonemes could also be of help—clearly discrediting the argument. Thus, the previously uttered phoneme "g" cannot in any way help the "o" to produce a special functional effect since it is dead and gone.[2]

Kumārila responds by putting forth yet another explanation. He offers the example of how the New and Full Moon sacrifices, along with other rites, have sequence and yet produce their effect together—as do the repeated saying of the *Veda* for its memorization. In such examples different acts occurring at different times are still found to produce qualitatively and numerically different effects. This same kind of process, he argues, should be accepted in the case of phonemes.[3] Maṇḍana

1. Sph., *Kārikā* 4 p., 11.

2. Unlike the subsequent discussion, the above debate assumes no invisible trace or *saṁskāra*. The last phoneme, helped by the mere visible going before of the other phonemes in the word, is held by Kumārila to cause the understanding of meaning.

3. See Sph., p. 14.

is quick to note, however, that though these examples may seem plausible they are not parallel to the case of the phonemes. In sequences such as the examples offered, where the resultant is unitary, thinkers agree that the new effect is due to a trace or lasting impression which each of the parts in the series leaves behind and which helps towards the one result. As Maṇḍana puts it, "In New and Full Moon sacrifices and the like, which have sequence, certain new elements (*apūrva*) which are produced by the acts and which last and are looked upon as powers or functions actually help (in producing the single effect)."[1] In the case of Vedic recitation, the final learning is achieved with the aid of the memory traces left by the preceding repetitions. In the case of both the sacrificial *apūrvas* and the memory traces, there is a kind of continuing existence or simultaneity which allows for cooperation among the serial instances towards a unitary result. However, Maṇḍana points out, this is clearly not possible in the case of the phonemes which were described above as leaving no trace.

Kumārila counters by allowing that phonemes may indeed leave lasting traces or impressions (*saṁskāras*), and through the traces left by the perceptions of the earlier phonemes and the last phoneme, the unity meaning of the word may be conveyed.[2] The last phoneme, when helped out by the *saṁskāras* of the previous phonemes, conveys the meaning.

Maṇḍana finds a fallacy in Kumārila's reasoning. Maṇḍana points out that *saṁskāras* which are generated by individual phonemes can only reinstate those same individual phonemes. The memory trace or *saṁskāra* for each phoneme will be present, but, just as in the case of the original utterance or hearing, only individually—when the "o" is uttered, or remembered, the *saṁskāra* for the "g" will have ceased to exist. There can only be the cognition of the phoneme at a time, and this principle applies equally to the *saṁskāra* and the original utterance or hearing of the phoneme. Thus, the possibility of the phonemes producing *saṁskāras* gets one no closer to accounting for the generation of a meaning-whole.[3]

---

1. See Sph., *Kārikā* 5, p. 15.
2. *Ibid.*, p. 16.
3. *Ibid.*, *Kārikā* 6, p. 16.

Kumārila defends his position by once again introducing an argument from "economy" (i.e., the position having to resort to the least numbers of postulated special powers or entities is best). Now it is agreed that each phoneme in both its original utterance or hearing or in its *saṁskāra* cannot co-exist with other phonemes so as to give the meaning of the word. Therefore, some cause for the occurrence of meaning must be postulated. The weakness of the *Sphoṭa* theory is that it has to make too many postulations : (1) it must postulate the existence of the *sphoṭa* as some kind of unseen entity, and (2) it must then impose upon this postulated *sphoṭa* the capacity to convey meaning. For the *Sphoṭa* theorist two things have to be postulated. The upholder of the phoneme, on the other hand, has to make only one additional postulation. As has already been made clear, the existence of the *saṁskāra* is accepted by both the disputants. The only point at issue is whether or not it can be the cause of the understanding of meaning. All that is needed, claims Kumārila, is that a new function be postulated for the *saṁskāra*, which everyone agrees exists. It is the cognition of the final phoneme, accompanied by the special function of the *saṁskāras* of the previous phonemes, that conveys the meaning. Thus only one additional postulation is required, the postulation of a new function for the *saṁskāras*. The *Sphoṭa* theorist is in an inferior position because he has to postulate both a new substance (i.e., the *sphoṭa*) and a new function (i.e., its ability to convey meaning).[1]

To Maṇḍana, Kumārila's explanation seems to be an over-simplification. The memory impression or *saṁskāra* is not seen but is a capacity or function which is inferred from the existence of the original phoneme. The difficulty comes when Kumārila postulates yet another function as resulting from the *saṁskāra* which is itself already an inferred function. Maṇḍana maintains that the postulation of functions etc., is unacceptable because it results in an infinite regress (*anavasthā*). In addition to this problem of infinite regress, Maṇḍana finds logical weaknesses in Kumārila's view that it is the cognition of the final phoneme, accompanied by the cognitions of the previous phonemes that conveys the meaning. This cannot hold, says

1. See Sph., *Kārikā* 6, pp. 17-18.

Maṇḍana, since the *saṁskāras* left by the letters are the same even when their order is reversed. How is it then that the meanings of the words "now" and "won" are not identical? Since the letters and *saṁskāras* involved in the two words are identical, their meanings should also be identical and this is clearly not the case.[1,2]

Letting go of this argument, Kumārila takes up his final and seemingly most potent line of attack. He returns to the proposition that the last phoneme, accompanied by the *saṁskāras* of the previous phonemes, expresses the meaning. To avoid the difficulties encountered above, he now defines *saṁskāra* not as a memory trace, but rather as "something else which is brought about by the cognition of the phonemes uttered separately in a fixed order by a particular speaker and leading to the understanding of meaning and it is similar to the effect called *apūrva* (residual force) brought about by the performance of the different rites like a sacrifice and leading to heaven."[3] The distinguishing feature of the *saṁskāra* which causes remembrance is that it causes something similar to that which produced it. This, however, is not the case of *apūrva* in a sacrifice. In a sacrifice, the individual acts performed perish immediately, but the *apūrva* or after-effect of the whole sacrifice inheres in the self of the sacrificer as a special kind of potency until it brings the reward of heaven. Its result is thus very different from its cause, and this unusual kind of causal relationship is necessitated by scripture's declaration that the performance of a sacrifice produces such a result. In Kumārila's view, the *apūrva* or after-effect kind of *saṁskāra* which is left by the different letters upon the subject is analogous to such religious leaven. Just as in a sacrifice it is the determinate order of performance

1. See Sph., *Kārikā* 7, p. 19.

2. For our present purposes, *Kārikas* 8 and 9 are omitted as obscure variations on the same argument stated in *Kārikā* 7. Whereas in *Kārikā* 7 Kumārila's position is that it is the cognition of the final phoneme accompanied by the *saṁskāras* of the previous phonemes that conveys the meaning, in *Kārikās* 8 and 9 a variant and rather obscure interpretation is given suggesting that all the phonemes *together* convey the meaning. Although this seems to allow for a kind of felt unity, it is open to the same objections regarding order of phonemes in relation to meaning that Maṇḍana marshalled against Kumārila's position in *Kārikā* 7. See G. Sastri, *Word*, pp. 109-111.

3. Sph., *Kārikā* 10, p. 30.

by a single agent that is responsible for the spiritual leaven, here also the determinate order of the phonemes uttered by a single person is responsible for the unusual result. So it is when the last phoneme being spoken or heard in the midst of the "leavening" effect of the *saṁskāras* of the previous phonemes that the meaning is conveyed.[1] For Kumārila, *śabda* is the last phoneme being heard or spoken and conveying the meaning (when helped by the *saṁskāras* of the previous phonemes). The exact nature of this help is that the *saṁskāras* of the previous phonemes become a kind of intermediate cause (*vyāpāra*).[2] They help the last phoneme in its task of conveying meaning. This does not depreciate the causal value of the previous phonemes in any way since it is in harmony with their purpose—the phonemes are not uttered just for the sake of pronouncing letters or leaving impressions, but also for the purpose of conveying a meaning.[3] This importance of and necessity for the phonemes as causing the conveyance of meaning must also be admitted by the proponent of the *sphoṭa* or indivisible word, Kumārila claims. The proponent of the *sphoṭa* or undivided word-entity has to admit that it is manifested by the phonemes uttered or heard in a definite order. As no single letter can be said to reveal the *sphoṭa*, it must then be revealed by all the phonemes combined with one another. Nor can it be that each phoneme in succession reveals only a part of the *sphoṭa* because the *sphoṭa*, by definition, is held to be a simple indivisible whole. For the very reasons given by the *Sphoṭa* theorist himself, the phonemes of a word existing in a fixed sequence have no way of pooling themselves or their *saṁskāras* so as to result in a unitary whole. Just as the *Mīmāṁsaka* has been forced to do, so also the *Sphoṭa* theorist is forced to have recourse to postulating some special kind of leaven of *saṁskāra* by means of which the phonemes reveal the whole meaning. Why then, asks Kumārila (recalling his "economy" principle once more), does he not attribute the conveying of meaning to a special *saṁskāra* function itself and leave out the extra step of postulation of a special kind of *saṁskāra and* the postulation of the *sphoṭa*.

1. See Sastri, *Word*, p. 112.
2. See Iyer, Doctrine, p. 130.
3 See Sph., *Kārikā* 10, p. 31.

For these reasons, concludes Kumārila, "it is better to assume that the special *saṁskāra* which has to be postulated conveys the meaning (rather than that it reveals the word)."[1]

Maṇḍana answers the above criticism by making clear that the *Sphoṭa* theory does not postulate a new kind of *apūrva* for the conveyance of meaning. *Sphoṭa* theory needs nothing more than the postulation of the ordinary *saṁskāra* or memory trace. It is just the commonly accepted *saṁskāras* (or *vāsanās*—dispositions) that result in the revelation of the *sphoṭa*. The only *new* thing postulated by *Sphoṭa* theory is the *sphoṭa* itself, and in fact even that need not be postulated because it is directly perceptible.[2] Now, maintains Maṇḍana, this is far superior to the position of Kumārila where the one new thing (i.e., the *apūrva* type *saṁskāra*) cannot be perceived and has to be postulated on the authority of scripture and on analogy to religious merit. Even this analogy is very weak since although the postulation of *apūrva* or religious merit is necessary to validate the moral law and religious rites, there is no such necessity in the apprehension of the word and its meaning. The cases are not parallel. Also ignored is the common man's intuition, "I understand the meaning from the word," and teaching of tradition that "the word, the meaning and their relation is eternal."[3] There is a natural connection between word and meaning which is inalienable. The conventions that we learn as children serve only to bring that relation out and to make the meaning present to us. Maṇḍana summarizes his rejection of Kumārila's position as follows : "Because it has been said that the impressions, after all, do not constitute the word, the final phoneme is not expressive, [therefore] a collection of phonemes does not constitute the word and it does not convey any meaning."[4]

Perhaps it would be helpful to pause here and outline the chief points made by each side in the argument.

1. See Sph. *Kārikā* 10, p. 31.
2. *Ibid.*, *Kārikā* 11, p. 34.
3. *Ibid.*
4. *Ibid.*

OUTLINE OF CHIEF POINTS IN THE ARGUMENT

Kumārila (*Mīmāṁsā*)	*Maṇḍana* (*Sphoṭa*)
1. *Śabda* refers to phoneme as uttered.	1. *Śabda* refers to *sphoṭa* or indivisible word-whole which is a felt-fact in common experience.
2. Phonemes cause the understanding of meaning when grouped together in the form of words (pada).	2. Because of their ubiquitous and eternal nature, phonemes (as defined by *Mīmāṁsakas*) can only exist singly and cannot possibly co-exist as *pada* so as to convey meaning. This inability of the phonemes to convey meanings points to the *sphoṭa* as the revealer of meaning.
3. Various suggestions as to how the phonemes could be grouped together so as to convey meaning :	3. Difficulties vitiating each suggestion :
(a) *e.g.*, *seed.* Just as a seed will produce a new effect (sprout) when helped by other factors, so also the phonemes when combined with a group of helping factors (such as being uttered by the same person in a particular sequence) will result in the conveying of meaning.	(a) How can being uttered by the same person in a particular sequence make the discrete phonemes c-o-w into a word when each letter vanishes completely before the subsequent one is uttered ?
(b) *via saṁskāras.* Phonemes leave memory traces so that the traces of the earlier phonemes together with the utterance of the	(b) *Saṁskāras,* like their original individual phonemes, have only discrete existences vanishing completely before subsequent ones come into

last phoneme conveys the meaning.	existence—therefore no possibility for grouping into a word or conveying meaning exists.
(c) *via apūrva.* Phonemes leave impressions different from the ones which cause remembrance, and are like *apūrva* in a sacrifice, where the unified result is different in nature from the individual causes (parts of the sacrifice). When spoken by a single person in a determinate order, the *apūrva* of the phonemes inheres in the self so that when the last phoneme is uttered the *śabda* is understood and its meaning conveyed.	(c) Analogy from the *apūrva* of religious merit (which is based on an inference from scripture so as to validate the moral law) to the *saṁskāras* of phonemes rendering them capable of conveying meaning is unjustifiable. Rather it is the case that the ordinary memory traces of the phonemes reveal the already existing inherent *sphoṭa* which provides awareness of the whole and determines the order of the phonemes.
4. In the above view 3 (c) only one new thing (i.e., the special *apūrva*-like power) need be postulated, whereas Maṇḍana postulates two or three new things—a special *saṁskāra* and a *sphoṭa* (and a special power of that *sphoṭa*—conveying of meaning).	4. Only new thing postulated is *sphoṭa* itself and even that need not be postulated since it is directly perceptible. *Saṁskāra* referred to is the common memory trace which has the same object as that of the uttered phoneme (i.e., the *sphoṭa*). The unified *sphoṭa* was the original cause of the phoneme and is the end-object of both it and its *saṁskāra*. Thus no special or illogical power, such as *apūrva* is postulated.

In this logical argument, it seems clear that Kumārila's attempt to identify *śabda* with the uttered phoneme is effectively discredited by the reasoning of Maṇḍana, who at the same time has vindicated the identification of *śabda* with *sphoṭa.* Although the logical groundwork has largely been completed, Maṇḍana still has to describe in detail exactly how *śabda* as *sphoṭa* may be comprehended using only ordinary memory traces of the phonemes to reveal the *sphoṭa*. He must also show the *sphoṭa* to be not a mere postulation but a perceivable reality, otherwise much of his logical argument simply collapses. These tasks he undertakes in *Kārikās* 18 and 19 of the *Sphoṭasiddhi*.

In his explanation Maṇḍana depends upon the basic concepts put forward by Bhartṛhari in Chapter I of his *Vākyapadiya*.[1] The *sphoṭa* is something over and above the phonemes. The phonemes are changeable (capable of variations such as accent, speed, etc.), and when uttered serve only to manifest the changeless *sphoṭa* which exists within the speaker and is potentially present within every hearer. The phonemes do not convey the meaning, but the *sphoṭa*, once manifested, conveys the meaning. Between the *sphoṭa* and its word-meaning aspect the relation is that of expression and thing or meaning expressed. This is a natural relationship which is indestructible and beginningless. Convention only serves to bring it out. Bhartṛhari emphasizes that the *sphoṭa* is an entity which is within each person. All of us have the capacity to instinctively feel its existence within, and ultimately to directly perceive it with the mind. The contention that the *sphoṭa* may be directly perceived, and is not merely a thing which is inferred, is one of the key points of *Sphoṭa* theory.[2] Keeping these basic concepts in mind, let us now examine Maṇḍana's detailed description of just how the *sphoṭa* is both cognized and perceived without recourse to any new *apūrva*-type postulations.

This process by which the *sphoṭa* is cognized is stated by Maṇḍana in his commentary on *Kārikā* 18 of the *Sphoṭasiddhi* as follows :

> Each sound individually reveals the whole *sphoṭa*. Nor do the other sounds thus become useless because there is a difference in the revelation. It is like this : All the previous sounds bring about in the listener whose mind is free from any particular residual impression [*saṁskāra*], cognitions in which the word figures vaguely and which sow seeds in the form

1. As Iyer notes, the thoughts put forward by Maṇḍana are not original but essentially a restatement of the ideas and analogies offered by Bhartṛhari in his *Vākyapadīya*, Chapter I, with the *Vṛtti*. See his "Introduction" to Sph., p. 10.

2. *Ibid.*

of residual impressions capable of producing a later clear cognition of the word. The last sound produces a clear cognition in which figures, as it were, clearly the image of the *sphoṭa* caused by all the seeds in the form of residual impressions left by the vague cognitions of the previous sounds.[1]

Maṇḍana offers the analogy of a jeweller who examines the genuineness of a precious stone. His continuous gaze is really a series of cognitions, each of which perceives the genuineness of the stone but with increasing clarity. Each cognition leaves its *saṁskāra* or common memory trace. The last cognition, helped by the *saṁskāra* of the previous ones, fully perceives the genuineness of the stone; but for the *saṁskāras* of the intervening cognitions, there would be no difference between the last one and the first one. An important point is that the jeweller is described as "expert," meaning that before beginning the examination he already had the image of a precious stone ingrained in his subconscious, and it was this image (like the inhering *sphoṭa*) which was revealed to the jeweller's mind by his series of partial perceptions.

The *sphoṭa* is a unity which already exists in the mind of the speaker. He utters sounds in order to manifest it and once manifested the *sphoṭa* conveys the meaning. A reasonable explanation of this process by which the *sphoṭa* and its meaning are held to be revealed is offered by Śeṣakṛṣṇa in his *Sphoṭatattva-nirūpaṇa*. As the phoneme "c" is spoken by someone intending to say "cow," the hearer grasps not only the phoneme "c" but also the whole word rather vaguely, since it is now known that the speaker is pronouncing a word beginning with "c" and not with any other sound. But there are a multitude of words beginning with "c" and we do not know which one is going to be uttered, thus the vagueness of our knowledge. However, when the speaker utters the next phoneme, "o," the field of possible words is further narrowed. All words not having "co" at the beginning are now excluded, and the hearer's knowledge of the whole is less vague. When the final phoneme, "w," is uttered, all doubt disappears as the "w" unites with the memory traces "co" to manifest the whole *sphoṭa* "cow," which immediately conveys its meaning.[2]

1. See Sph., *Kārikā* 18, p. 44.
2. See Iyer, "Doctrine," p. 136.

The above explanation makes clear the reason behind Maṇḍana's insistence that a speaker's efforts to utter the phonemes will differ according to the *sphoṭa* which he wants to manifest. Even though the phoneme may be the same (e.g., the "w" in "won" and "now"), the physical effort involved in vocalizing it will vary according to the position it occupies in the word. Thus the overall physical effort in saying "won" will be markedly different from that involved in saying "now", even though the same three phonemes are involved in each case. Consequently, the *Sphoṭa* theorist has a basis for claiming that the *sphoṭas* manifested by the two vocalizations would be different, as would the meanings revealed.[1]

This last point is important in relation to the *Mīmāṁsaka* contention that since the phonemes are changeless no mere difference in order or effort of vocalization can be important factors in the production of different meanings. Therefore, according to the *Mīmāṁsaka*, were it not for the postulation of the special "*apūrva*-like effect," the same meaning should result from "now" and "won." From the *Sphoṭa* viewpoint, however, it is the *sphoṭa* which is changeless and not the phoneme, and the evident variations in the pronunciation and ordering of phonemes in speaking different words is seen to be consistent with both *Sphoṭa* theory and the evidence of experience. "Now" and "won" are composed of the same three phonemes but do require that the vocalization of those phonemes be given different orders and intentions or efforts for the appropriate *sphoṭa* to be manifested and its meaning revealed.

The strength of this *Sphoṭa* explanation as to how the word-meaning is revealed rests not only on its concurrence with experience but also on the fact that no new kind of *saṁskāra* is postulated. The *saṁskāra* employed is the usual trace providing for the remembrance of the phoneme which originally caused it. "The weak point of the *Mīmāṁsaka* explanation," as Iyer puts it, "was that it either postulated a new power for the ordinary kind of residual trace, or postulated a new kind of residual trace in order to explain the fact that, though caused by the cognition of the sound, it does not stop at causing a remembrance of it but causes the understanding of the meaning

1. See Sph., p. 12.

also."[1] In other words, the *saṁskāra* is supposed to have an object different from that of the cognition which deposited it in the first place, and this, says the *Sphoṭa* theorist, is a logical impossibility. In his case, the original *sphoṭa* (which lay behind the vocalization of the phonemes by the speaker) and the end *sphoṭa* (which is the object of both the uttered phonemes and their *saṁskāras*) are one and the same. Consequently, the object (i.e., the *sphoṭa*) of the phonemes and the *saṁskāras* is identical, and there is no logical difficulty of the kind which besets the *Mīmāṁsaka*.

Another aspect of the *Sphoṭa* explanation, which is emphasized both in the *Vṛtti* on *Vākyapadiya* I:89 and by Maṇḍana in his comment on *Kārikā* 19 of the *Sphoṭasiddhi*, is that the final clear perception of the *sphoṭa* is achieved through a series of errors. The analogy is offered of how from a distance one (if one is in India) may mistake a tree for an elephant, but if one keeps on looking at it, the tree is ultimately recognized in its true form. In this situation the truth has been arrived at through a series of errors. The sense organ (in this case the eye) has been in contact with the tree throughout. The errors of perception have had the tree as their object, but the cognitions produced by the eye have had an elephant as their form. When, however, the final or true cognition takes place, it has the form of the tree itself and is one with its object. But this true cognition has been arrived at by going through the series of erroneous perceptions that preceded it. Now this change from error to true perception cannot be explained by factors such as change in distance, since simply standing in the same spot and gazing with intense concentration often produces the described result. According to Maṇḍana, "it is the previous cognitions (having tree as the object and the form of an elephant) leaving progressively clearer residual impressions, which become the cause of the clear perception of the tree.[2] There could have been no erroneous cognition of elephant had the tree not been there as an object for the sense organ to come into contact with in the first place. The error, therefore, may

1. See Sph., p. 12, Iyer's "Introduction," p. 13.

2. *Ibid.*, *Kārikā* 19. Similar arguments are offered to show how the progressively clearer perception cannot be attributed to defects of the senses or memory through resemblance, p. 49.

be described as misapprehension or vague perception. In the context of our discussion about words, the *sphoṭa* is similarly said to be the object of the cognitions of each of the phonemes and yet it at first appears in the form of the phoneme. Through the additional cognitions of the subsequent phonemes, however, the *sphoṭa* is seen with increasing clarity until with the uttering of the final phoneme the form of the phonemes has become identical with that of the *sphoṭa*. Here the phonemes are seen in a position which at first glance seems parallel to the snake in the famous rope-snake illusion of *Advaita Vedānta*. The perception of the rope as snake is error, but it is through the negating of the erroneous snake-perception that the true rope-perception is finally realized. Were it not for the prior existence of the rope, the erroneous perception would have lacked the necessary ground for its phenomenal existence. Similarly, in this case, the phonemes are seen as dependent upon the *sphoṭa* for their phenomenal existence, but in that phenomenal existence as being the means by which the noumenal *sphoṭa* may be perceived. This apparent parallelism, however, does not hold up under closer analysis. As noted previously, *Advaita* theory provides for only true or false cognitions and allows no progressive approximation to the real, as is the case in a series of erroneous *sphoṭa* perceptions. Whereas the Advaitin describes his error as being transcended via a single negation (e.g., as when it is realized "this is not snake"), the Grammarian holds that his error (e.g., the vagueness of the perception of the whole in the first phoneme) is positively overcome by the increasingly clear perception of the *sphoṭa* which the succeeding phonemes reveal. This analysis of how error is overcome would seem to give further weight to Sastri's suggestion, noted above, that in some ways the doctrine of reflection (*ābhāsa*) of the Kashmir *Trika* writers may provide the closest parallel to *Sphoṭa* theory. In the Kashmir *Trika* view consciousness (*caitanya*) is the only reality, and all external manifestation is held to be a reflection on consciousness as on a mirror. Error, in this view, occurs not because the initial perception has no existence, but because its reflection of the object captures or includes only a part of its totality and adds in other material (*saṁskāras*) taken from the old stock of memory. This error is positively transcended as the form of the reflection is progressively purified of memory material until it perfectly reflects the object. This perfect reflection, which is true knowledge, is further described as a union of the subjective and objective aspects of consciousness—a return to the oneness which is its essential nature.[1] From this brief glance at the Kashmir *ābhāsa* theory, it would seem to provide a helpful parallel supporting the *Sphoṭa* view of the way in which the manifest phonemes erroneously but positively approximate their true object, the *sphoṭa* itself. Of course it may also be the case that *Sphoṭa* Theory influenced Kashmir Śaivism, in which case the notion of "parallels" would not apply.

Returning to Maṇḍana, his explanation of the paradox as to how the indivisible *sphoṭa* appears as the phonemes, and the phonemes as the parts of the partless *sphoṭa* is as follows. He says it is the sounds that resemble one another which are the cause of both the error and the final correct cognition of the *sphoṭa*. If, for the manifestation of two different word-*sphoṭas*, one has to make similar movements of the vocal organs, the phonemes produced by these movements appear to be parts of both of the indivisible words.[2] This is an error which is fostered by the construction of such artificial devices as alphabet letters or word syllables, usually for teaching purposes. It is precisely because of this kind of confusion, says Maṇḍana, that sentences, words, and phonemes appear to have parts whereas in reality they have none.[3] The obverse of this applies to the *sphoṭa*. From the phenomenal viewpoint the *sphoṭa* "cow," for example, may appear to possess qualities such as accent, speed, loudness, time, place and person in its utterance. That these are qualities of the phenomenal sounds and not the noumenal *sphoṭa* is what makes possible the common recognition of the word "cow" in spite of its diversity of utterance. From the *Sphoṭa* viewpoint, it is this noumenal grounding or basis that makes possible such things as the translation of thought from one phenomenal language to another.

A subsequent scholar of considerable note, Vācaspati Miśra, attempts to reject Maṇḍana's conception of the relation between

1. See K. C. Pandey, *Abhinavagupta*. The *ābhāsa* theory is summarized on pp. 400-427.

2. *Sphoṭasiddhi*, Kārikā 20, and *Vākyapadīya* I:88, "Vṛtti."

3. *Ibid.*

the phonemes and the *sphoṭa*.[1] This criticism occurs in its fullest form in Vācaspati's *Tattvabindu*. The argument is stated as follows : "The particular sounds which manifest *Sphoṭa*, are they different from *Sphoṭa* or non-different therefrom ?"[2] If non-different, says Vācaspati, then each phoneme should manifest the *sphoṭa* and the remaining phonemes would be futile. If different, then there is no ground for the relating of the phonemes to the manifestation of the *sphoṭa*. If the phonemes are treated as illusory, then their reality is discredited—yet in experience we undoubtedly cognize individual letters. What is the justification for treating such cognitions as illusory ?

In supporting the *Sphoṭa* argument of Maṇḍana, S. S. S. Sastri effectively answers these criticisms of Vācaspati as follows. To the criticisms regarding difference and non-difference Sastri replies,

> Such a question has little application to Maṇḍana's doctrine. To him indeed *Sphoṭa* is non-different from the sounds, as a whole is from its parts; and yet it is different too, since the whole is neither each part nor a mere aggregate of parts. The existence and functioning of such wholes can only be denied by defective psychology.[3]

As regards the justification for treating cognitions of the phonemes as illusory, Sastri answers :

> The obvious reply is that not the existence of these cognitions but their significance is in question, just as in the case of the reflection. The reflection exists without doubt, but it is not real. And sublation in this case consists not in that presentation ceasing to be or giving place to another presentation, but in that presentation *as such* failing to fulfil what is

1. It should perhaps be noted here that no less a person than *Śaṅkara* argued against the *Sphoṭa* theory (Ś.B.B.S. I, 3.28). See also the recent analysis of *Śaṅkara's* objection to *Sphoṭa* by A. L. Herman, "Sphoṭa," in *Journal of the Ganganatha Jha Research Institute* 19, (1963), pp. 1-21. *Śaṅkara* and Kumārila both base their criticism on *ācārya* Upavarṣa, and their objections are somewhat different from the debate between Vācaspati and Maṇḍana.

2. This and the following sentences are taken from the translation by S. S. S. Sastri in his article "Vācaspati's Criticism of Sphoṭa-Vāda," in *Collected Papers of S. S. Suryanarayana Sastri*. (Madras : University of Madras, 1961), p. 296.

3. *Ibid*.

> expected of it. If each cognition as an independent part could by combination with other such parts explain the whole, then it would be unsublated; since, however, it fails of its purpose, since it seems to fit in more naturally with a theory which treats it not as a producer but as manifester, it is in so far forth sublated. The reflection is sublated not as a reflection, but as the face; the letter-cognition is sublated not as letter-cognition but as an independent productive constituent of meaning.[1]

Sastri observes that Vācaspati adopts and attempts to further develop Kumārila's viewpoint by trying to show that meaning somehow results from the phonemes entering into a single memory. As Sastri points out, however, such an explanation is untenable in the light of experience. If "cowness" is associated with the remembered letters "c," "o," "w," that meaning should not be recalled except when all three letters are present. How is it then that when there is a misprint such as "coe" or a mispronunciation such as "coo" we still correctly apprehend the meaning to be "cow ?" The same sort of thing is evident when a letter or sound is omitted in the course of writing or speaking. The explanation in all of these situations would seem to be that we do not pass from part to part but rather apprehend the whole filling up gaps or correcting errors when they occur.[2]

With regard to memory and sequence, Vācaspati, following Kumārila, maintains that in the memory itself the phonemes have no sequence being presented together, but memory follows experience, conforms to it, and the sequence in which the letters are experienced are repeated in memory. This contention, however, does not square with the view that letters, being eternal and pervasive, can have no sequence belonging to themselves. This difficulty is overcome in the *Sphoṭa* view which holds that the sequence is determined by something other than the letters—the *sphoṭa* intended. It is not the case that the letters in sequence constitute the word, rather, it is the word or *sphoṭa* that determines the sequence. The question may then be asked : is the word existent or non-existent prior to the

1. *Collected Papers of S.S. Suryanarayana Sastri*, p. 296.
2. *Ibid.*, p. 300.

phonemes being apprehended in sequence? In purely empirical terms, the question may be shelved by saying that though not present in my mind before I learn the sequence, it is present in the mind of another who instructs me; and in this fashion the process may be pushed further and further back, there being no authority for postulating the origin of language at any particular time. But such empirical indefiniteness does not seem adequate in the face of the common ground which necessarily appears to underlie all empirical languages—requiring the *sphoṭa* interpretation that the word both is and is not prior to the apprehension of sequence. This paradox is ridiculed by Vācaspati who describes it as the *Sphoṭa* claim that the unreal helps the real. Sastri, in answer, states the *Sphoṭa* argument, "It is real, otherwise it could not be manifested in sequence; it is not existent, otherwise there would be no need for manifestation."[1] This solution, Sastri observes, is in line with the solution of the problems of human knowledge and activity in general. "Knowledge is of the novel and yet not of the non-existent. Activity realizes a purpose which is real yet not actual."[2] As both the *Advaita Vedānta* and the *Sphoṭa* theorists point out, the only solution to this paradox, which seems to be universally present in human experience, would seem to be the taking of the phenomenal as partial and therefore defective and illusory appearances of the unitary real. It is from this viewpoint that *Sphoṭa* theory claims there is a given whole (i.e., *sphoṭa*) which is increasingly revealed by particular phonemes uttered in sequence. As Sastri concisely puts it, "The succeeding sounds make more clear what was less clearly expressed by the preceding sounds; the latter provides the substructure, the former superstructure, while all of them together reveal the one design, which while prompting their utterance is certainly not produced by them."[3]

The same paradox is described by Maṇḍana in his analysis of the relation between the universal and the particular. When one perceives the universal of an object, we perceive the particular and its qualities also, yet the essential, cognition is that of

1. *Collected Papers of S.S. Suryanarayana Sastri*, p. 301.
2. *Ibid.*
3. *Ibid.*, p. 293.

the universal. To put it another way, when the cognition of the whole takes place we are also aware of the parts which make up the whole, but it is the cognition of the whole which is dominant.[1] Maṇḍana offers the example of a picture. He points out that in our cognition of a picture, although we may be aware of the different parts and colours, the picture is perceived as a whole which is over and above its parts.[2] Similarly, when we perceive a piece of cloth our cognition is of the cloth as a whole and is quite distinct from the particular threads and colours involved.[3]

In both of these examples there is a necessary perception of the parts prior to the perception of the whole. This aspect is brought out clearly by Bhartṛhari who describes the painter

1. See Iyer's introduction to Sph., p. 17.

2. *Ibid.*, *Kārikā* 24, p. 64. See also K. A. S. Iyer's article, "The Conception of Guṇa Among the Vaiyyākaraṇas," in which he makes clear that from the *Sphoṭa* viewpoint whatever distinction of degree or part is made in an object must be done through a *guṇa* (quality of particular). For the Grammarians it is the *guṇa* and never the universal which serves to express degrees in objects. *New Indian Antiquary* V(6), pp. 121-130.

It should also be noted that of the many possible ways of interpreting the universal, Bhartṛhari prefers the following. A movement like lifting the hand consists of a series of movements. As these movements are transitory they cannot co-exist and form a whole of which they would be the parts and in which the universal of the movement of lifting the hand would inhere. Now such a universal is more specific than the wider universal of movement in general. Although it inheres in each moment of movement, it is not capable of being cognized in them alone due to too much similarity between moments of lifting and those of the moments of other movements such as turning the hand. The moments of each movement are the result of a special effort to make that movement and they are the substrata of the universal of that movement. But that universal cannot be cognized until a series of moments has been cognized. One or two moments of movement are not enough, but after a series of moments is cognized the cognition of the universal inherent in each moment becomes clear. Lifting, for example, may be identified and other movements such as turning excluded. The process is similar in the manifestation of *sphoṭas*. Each is manifested by a series of special efforts to utter phonemes. One or two utterances of the series are not enough to eliminate other words with similar sounds. But as the complete series of phonemes is cognized, the cognition of the *sphoṭa* or universal of the particular word is clearly perceived and meaningful usage of it in speech becomes possible. See Vāk. II:20-21 as interpreted by D. A. S. Iyer in *Bhartṛhari*, pp. 168-169.

3. *Ibid.*

as going through three stages when he paints a picture : "When a painter wishes to paint a figure having parts like that of a man, he first sees it gradually in a sequence, then as the object of a single cognition and then paints it on cloth or on a wall in sequence."[1] So also the hearer of a word perceives the word in a sequence of phonemes which manifest in him the whole word as the object of a single cognition. As a speaker, however, he utters the whole word in its differentiated appearance as a sequence of phonemes. It is in this context that the perception of the many phonemes, before the final perception of the unitary *sphoṭa*, is described as error, illusion or appearance. It is a unique kind of error, however, in that it has a fixed sequence and form, ultimately leads to the perception of the truth, and is thus regarded as a universal error.[2] The chief cause of this universal error is described as *avidyā* or the limitation which is individual self-consciousness. A characteristic of this *avidyā* is that it provides no other means for cognizing the *sphoṭa*, except the phonemes. That is why all individual selves universally experience the same error with regard to speech; but, it is an error which ultimately leads to cognition of truth. It is only through this error or appearance of differentiation that the individual *sphoṭa* comes within the range of worldly usage so that we ordinary mortals have a way of comprehending it.[3] To illustrate this point, both Bhartṛhari and Maṇḍana make reference to the *Vaiśeṣika* conception that when two things are brought before us we first perceive each on separately and only on the basis of these separate perceptions does the notion of two arise. This is true for all higher numbers—their cognition and production is possible only by way of previously cognized lower numbers. So also it is by way of the lower differentiated forms of speech that the higher unities, the word-*sphoṭas*, may be understood.[4]

---

1. Vāk., I:52, p. 59.

2. If one moves beyond Sanskrit itself and into the world of languages, I would take the universal error as referring to the necessity of going from the differentiated phonemes (the error) to the whole *sphoṭa* (meaning or ultimate reality). The fixed sequence and form of the differentiation for a particular word-*sphoṭa* would only be a constant error within each language (such as Sanskrit).

3. See Vāk., I:85, p. 86.

4. *Ibid.*, I:87, p. 87, and Sph., *Kārikā* 21, p. 53.

Reference has been made to the apparent parallel between the *Sphoṭa* and *Advaita Vedānta* views of error; however, a significant difference in interpretation was seen to exist. Whereas the Advaitin usually describes the error as being transcended via negation (e.g., as when it is said "this is not snake"), the Grammarian holds that the error (e.g., the vagueness of the perception of the whole in the first phoneme) is positively overcome by the increasingly clear cognition of the *sphoṭa* which the succeeding phonemes reveal.[1] In addition, the final clear cognition is a case of perfect perception or *pratibhā* which, as will be shown in Chapter Seven is seen by the Grammarian as synonymous with *Veda* and the third or *paśyantī* stage of speech.[2] At the more mundane level of psychological functioning, however, the positive process of perfecting the perception is described by Iyer as follows :

> [The final] clear cognition is a case of perception. The previous cognitions also had the sphoṭa as their object, but the cognition of it was vague and that is why they had the form of the sounds... But when the final cognition reveals the sphoṭa in all its clarity and distinctness, it no longer has the form of sounds. The error has given place to truth. Such a cognition can only be perception. The object and forms of the cognition are now identical.[3]

This conformity between the object and the form of the cognition is referred to by Bhartṛhari as a certain fitness (*yogyatā*), between the sounds and the *sphoṭa* which results in the clear manifestation of the word.[4] The perfect perception in which there is identity between the object (i.e., the *sphoṭa*) and the form of its cognition (i.e., the phonemes or sounds) is a special kind of perception which—the modern reader must realize—is held

1. See Vāk., I:87, p. 87, and Sph., *Kārikā* 22, pp. 58-59.
2. See Kaviraj, *Pratibhā*, p. 14.
3. See Iyer's introduction to Sph., p. 26.
4. See Vāk., I:78-I:84, pp. 81-85. Among the analogies offered to explain the process, Bhartṛhari's favourite seems to be that the sounds leave impression-seeds (*saṁskāra-bīja*), which, as they mature in the mind, are *conductive* to an increasingly clear perception of the *sphoṭa*—to which they finally offer a perfect "fitness" or identity. A literal rendering of *yogyatā* could be "to fit in a frame"—the "fit" of the "matured" series of phonemes into the "frame" of the *sphoṭa*. See also *Vṛtti* on Vāk., III:1:8, p. 12.

to be a function of the mind[1] rather than the external sense organs. It is pertinent to note in the context of this philosophical analysis that the designation of the final cognition of the *sphoṭa* as a case of *perception* rather than *inference* has important logical implications.[2] Maṇḍana puts the point clearly :

> The revelation (of an object) clearly or vaguely is confined to direct perception. In the case of the other means of knowledge there is either apprehension (of the object) or not at all.[3]

According to almost all Schools of Indian Philosophy, the valid means of knowledge (*pramāṇas*), other than perception, either reveal the object completely or do not reveal it at all. There can be increasing degrees of knowledge only in the case of perception. This is most important for *Sphoṭa* theory in its contention that the error due to the vagueness of perception of the initial phonemes may be gradually and positively overcome, as described above. It is also crucial for the *Sphoṭa* theory in its contention that the existence of the *sphoṭa* is not a postulation, as the *Mīmāṁsakas* maintain, but is proven by direct perception.

Relation between sphoṭa and word-meaning

The above debate between Kumārila and Maṇḍana has concentrated primarily on the nature of the relationship between the parts or phonemes and the word as an uttered whole. In Maṇḍana's *Sphoṭasiddhi*, the way in which the external word-sounds manifest the unitary *sphoṭa* has been the point of focus. Throughout it has been assumed that once the *sphoṭa* is revealed the word-meaning is also known, due to a natural and indestructible relationship between the two. Maṇḍana seems to do

---

1. The phrase "function of the mind" here is intended to indicate that *pratibhā* is not a function of the ordinary senses (of the *Buddhi* stage of consciousness), but is characteristic of the pre-*buddhi* or *śabdatattva* stage.

2. It should be clearly understood here that perfect perception or *pratibhā*, however valid in itself, remains outside the realm of *pramāṇa* (which is characterized by *sensory* perception and *discursive* cognition). With regard to language, therefore, it is *sphoṭa* when manifested as speech that is *pramāṇa* (and not *sphoṭa* at the unified level of *pratibhā*). The point made above, however, still stands. The cognition of *sphoṭa* at the level of either *śabda pramāṇa* or *pratibhā* is via direct perception rather than inference.

3. See Sph., *Kārikā* 23, p. 60.

little more than affirm that this is indeed the case, and that it is self-evident in our experience.[1] Here Maṇḍana seems to be depending on Bhartṛhari's argument in the *Vākyapadīya*. Indeed, this aspect of the *Sphoṭa* theory, the relation between the *sphoṭa* and the word-meaning, receives major attention in Chapter Three, Part One of the *Vākyapadīya*. Bhartṛhari begins by pointing out that unless there is a relation between the word and its meaning, any word would convey any meaning—but that does not happen in experience. He maintains that when words are uttered three things are understood : (1) their own form (the uttered series of phonemes), (2) their meaning, and (3) the intention of the speaker. The relationship between these three he holds to be fixed and not created by man.[2] Of these three, the first can sometimes be cognized without the other two (e.g., as in the case of the child who can hear and correctly repeat or imitate the form of the word even though he has no notion of its meaning or of the meaning intended by the speaker). This own-form is said to be closest to the *sphoṭa* (*antaraṅga*); it is never apart from the *sphoṭa* and is distinct for each *sphoṭa*. The relation between the first and second aspects, the own-form and the meaning, is characterized "natural fitness" or *yogyatā* (referred to previously as the "fitting" of the sounds into the "frame" of the *sphoṭa*), and is described by Bhartṛhari as the relation of the expression and the meaning or thing expressed (*vācya-vācakabhāva*).[3] Iyer has drawn attention to the fact that the relations between the own-form and the *sphoṭa*, and the own-form and the meaning, are both described as *yogyatā* or natural fitness. Thus, the own-form is also looked upon as a *vācya* (that which is expressed). Of course as soon as it is understood, it becomes *vācaka* or expressive of the meaning, but in the first instance it is *vācya*—the own-form which conveys the meaning, yet which is also illuminated by the meaning.[4] Between the third aspect, the speaker's intention, and the *sphoṭa* there is a relation of cause and effect (*kāryakāraṇabhāva*).[5] This relation accounts for the fact that the uttered

1. See, for example, Sph., *Kārikās* 11, 18 and 19.
2. See Vāk., III.3.1, p. 76.
3. *Ibid.*
4. See Vāk., III.3.1.
5. See Iyer, *Bhartṛhari*, p. 204.

word brings to the listener's mind the idea which the speaker intended to communicate. The speaker's initial idea, therefore, is said to be the cause of the phonemes uttered which are in turn heard by the listener and result in the arising of a similar idea in his mind. In this sense of causal relation, the word and the meaning can be alternately viewed as cause or effect.[1]

Bhartṛhari attempts to further clarify the above relations, which he finds to exist intertwined within the *sphoṭa*, by offering helpful illustrations.[2] Iyer paraphrases Bhartṛhari as follows :

> It is not merely words which, because of a natural fitness, brings things to the mind, that is, cause knowledge. The senses also do it. Mention must be made of the signs also which cause inferential knowledge. But there is a difference between these three things. The senses are only a means in the production of knowledge. They do not form part of the knowledge itself. They are themselves not cognized while they produce cognition. They resemble words in one important aspect, namely, that they cause cognition through a natural fitness. As for signs, they do, like smoke in the inference of fire, enter into the cognition which they cause but stand apart from the thing cognized. The word, on the other hand, is not a mere cause of the cognition which it produces. The thing cognized appears to be one with the word itself.[3,4]

1. See Iyer, *Bhartṛhari*, p. 204.
2. See Vāk., III.3.2, p. 77.
3. Iyer, *Bhartṛhari*, p. 205.
4. It is of interest to note here that the distinction between "sign" and "symbol" or "*sphoṭa*" has relevance to much current debate. Cassirer, for example, also distinguishes between the two in terms of relations : a sign is related to the thing to which it refers in a fixed and unique way; a symbol, on the other hand, is extremely variable allowing, for example, the expression of the same meaning in various languages. See E. Cassirer, *An Essay on Man*, p. 40. Blanshard, however, opposes Cassirer by finding no basic difference between sign and symbol both of which he finds to be related to their object in a purely utilitarian fashion. The only distinction between the two is a purely psychological difference in the greater volume of associations amassed by the one so that it comes to be called "symbol." Blanshard, "Symbolism," in *Religious Experience and Truth*, ed. S. Hook. p. 50. Yet another recent thinker, Tillich, disagrees with both Cassirer and Blanshard. For Tillich, the sign is interchangeable at will and is impotent in itself. The symbol, however, has a necessary character and has power and meaning inherent

The concept of the natural fitness of *sphoṭa* is further defined, this time in relation to learning and convention. Bhartṛhari holds that this natural fitness or ability to convey a meaning is inherent in the word and made known to us through convention (*saṅketa*).[1] Convention here is understood as learning through observation of the use of words by others, particularly one's elders. The usage of words by the elders, and one's learning of that usage, is not a human creation but only a making present to ourselves of the existing natural capacity of words to convey meaning. This is what is meant by the "natural fitness" in the relation between *sphoṭa* and meaning. It implies (as does the relation of causality) that ultimately the meaning and the *sphoṭa* are seen as being identical. As Iyer puts it, "Both the word and the object meant are designated by the same word. If the word which brings the object to mind is *ghaṭa*, the object is also *ghaṭa*. One can go further and say that the cognition which the word produces is also *ghaṭa*."[2] The word and the meaning are identified, and the nature of such a paradoxical unity in diversity is termed *adhyāsa*—a superimposition of the various aspects or relations within the *sphoṭa* upon one another and upon the *sphoṭa* itself.[3,4]

Yet another characteristic which Bhartṛhari uses to describe the relation between the *sphoṭa* and word-meaning is that it is eternal. The nature of this eternality is something similar to that of the universal concept "jar-ness" which remains regardless

---

within it. P. Tillich, "The Religious Symbol," in *Religious Experience and Truth*, *ibid.*, p. 302. While Tillich's view of symbol may have apparent similarity with Bhartṛhari's conception of *sphoṭa*, it is evident that their conceptions of sign are quite different. Indeed, the Grammarian viewpoint on this problem seems to have a logic and appeal to experience which is absent from many of the modern views, and therefore should perhaps be seriously examined for contributions to the current debate.

1. See Vāk., III.3.2.
2. Iyer, *Bhartṛhari*, p. 205.
3. Vāk., III.3.1, p. 76.
4. At this point it should be noted that the meaning relation always exists with the correct form of the word, and never with its corrupt forms. Corrupt forms of words are described as not expressive of meaning. They only enable one to infer meaning from the correct form. This is also held to be the case with gestures—they are not themselves expressive but serve to invoke in the mind of the observer the correct word form which directly conveys the meaning. See Iyer, *Bhartṛhari*, p. 207.

of how many individual jars are destroyed. An individual jar may be destroyed, but the "jarness" which existed in it is eternal and continues to exist in other jars. The unchanging stream of continuity is its eternality. So also a *sphoṭa* may be manifest in a vast variety of utterances, yet the meaning-universal of that *sphoṭa* does not change or perish and in that sense is eternal. Nor is it necessary, for this view of eternality, that there should always exist an object corresponding to the meaning in the external world. Take, for example, the word *alāta-cakra* or "fire-wheel" (the illusion created by quickly rotating a torch in a circle). Although there is no corresponding object in the external world, the fact that the word "fire-wheel" invariably brings its meaning to mind constitutes its eternality. "The very fact that a meaning invariably comes to the mind whether an object corresponding to it is present or not is taken as a proof that the relation between the word and the meaning is eternal."[1]

Now if the meaning is something which invariably comes to one's mind when the *sphoṭa* is spoken—even though a corresponding object may not exist in the external world—then the meaning must be primarily mental in its ontological status. Indeed Bhartṛhari makes a distinction between the existence of an object in the external world (primary being), and the mental existence of a meaning in relation to a *sphoṭa* (secondary being). Words move in the realm of "secondary being," and within this realm may convey meaning whether they have anything corresponding to them in the outside world or not. The basic point here is that as soon as a word-meaning is cognized it has a kind of cognitive being, which must differ from primary being if a sentence such as "The tree exists" is to be intelligible. Such a sentence would mean that the tree which has cognitive being in our mind or thought also exists or has primary being in the external world as well. So also, "The tree does not exist" would mean that the tree which is cognized in thought has no primary being in the external world. This distinction between primary and secondary being, Bhartṛhari takes from Patañjali's statement in the *Mahābhāṣya* on *Pāṇini Sūtra* 5.2.94, "no meaning of a word is without this (Secondary) Being."[2]

1. Iyer, *Bhartṛhari*, p. 208.
2. As quoted by Iyer in *Bhartṛhari*, p. 211.

The *Vṛtti* on *Vākyapadīya* III.3.1 makes clear that throughout the above discussion on the relation between *sphoṭa* and meaning, it is really *sphoṭa* as sentence rather than word that the Grammarian intends. Indeed, as Iyer suggests, all this effort—especially on the part of Maṇḍana—to prove the existence of the word-*sphoṭa* as the entity over and above the phonemes might lead one to think that he believes in the ultimate reality of it. However, he probably did it only for the benefit of the *Mīmāṁsaka*, especially Kumārila, who had identified the word with the smallest element of speech, the phoneme. But throughout, "He was aware that all the arguments by which he sought to prove that the phonemes by themselves cannot convey the meaning ... could be used to show that the words also cannot convey the meaning and that another entity, higher than words, namely, the sentence must be postulated to explain how we understand the meaning when we hear somebody speak."[1] Let us therefore now examine the *sphoṭa* as sentence.

Sphoṭa and Sentence-Meaning (*Vākya-Sphoṭa*)

The above analysis of the argument regarding *sphoṭa* and word-meaning has laid bare the logical basis of the *sphoṭa* position—meaning is conveyed by the whole and not by the summation of the parts; and for *Sphoṭa* theory it is the sentence which is taken to be the primary whole in language. Bhartṛhari bases his viewpoint not just on logical argument,[2] but on the

---

1. Iyer, "Doctrine," p. 146.

2. If one develops the *Sphoṭa* position purely in terms of logical consistency, a monistic hierarchy such as the following necessarily results. Just as the phonemes are only unreal abstractions of the word, so also words are unreal abstractions of the sentence and sentences unreal abstractions of the paragraph. Even the paragraph is not the ultimate unity, since it is only an unreal division of the chapter of the book. At the top of this language hierarchy perhaps there is only one indivisible reality within our literary self which, due to our human ignorance, limitation or *avidyā*, can only manifest itself in such unreal forms as the book, the chapter, the paragraph, the sentence and the word. The underlying principle, maintains Bhartṛhari, is that all difference presupposes a unity. Where there is difference or parts there must be an underlying identity, otherwise the one could not be related to the other and each would constitute a word by itself. This is the grounding for Bhartṛhari's metaphysical speculation. Our literary life is only a part of our total life, which all may simply be the manifestation of one central, eternal and indivisible principle—*Śabda Brahman* or *Parā Vāk*, having the *Praṇava* as its mystic unitary utterance. See Vāk., I:1 and I:9; Iyer, "Doctrine." p. 147; Murti, "Some Thoughts," pp. 18-19

observation that in common everyday language people speak in sentence units rather than individual words. He is convinced that the chief reality in linguistic communication is the indivisible sentence and sentence-meaning (*vākya-sphoṭa*). Although within his hierarchcial theory he can speak of the phoneme (*varṇa*) and the individual word (*pada*) as meaning bearing units (*sphoṭa*), the main form of the latter is the sentence.[1] In *kāṇḍa* two of the *Vākyapadiya*, Bhartṛhari establishes this position reference to two ancient scholars, Vārttākṣa and Audumbarāyaṇa, whose rejection of the fourfold classification of words as parts of speech he adduces in support of the unitary reality of the sentence.[2] Bhartṛhari also refers to Yāska's *Nirukta* and, according to one scholar, shows him to be in agreement with Audumbarāyaṇa's view that it is the sentence-meaning as a whole which exists in the mind of the hearer, and therefore the existence of four parts of speech is denied.[3]

Everyday communication is achieved through sentences which the speaker has in his mind and which he evokes in the mind of the hearer. Regardless of whether such sentences are fact or fiction, they exist as unities. In the mind of the speaker as he begins to speak the sentence-*sphoṭa* assumes two aspects : the sentence-sounds or component words, and the expressed sentence-meaning. Only as the hearer hears all of the words of the sentences in conjunction with their vague meanings does the realization of the sentence-meaning (*vākya-sphoṭa*) burst forth as a flash of intuition (*pratibhā*). This sentence-meaning is quite different from the meanings of the individual words which in the end are seen to have no ultimate reality in themselves. As the words of a sentence are heard one understands their meanings in a particular manner, but when the whole sentence is grasped by the mind the meaning appears to be quite different. This occurs, for example, in the case of a sentence in which the meanings of many words seem to be understood only to be completely changed by a negation at the end. Thus one cannot take the meanings of the individual words seriously until the whole sentence is heard, and then it is

1. Iyer, *Bhartṛhari*, p. 182.
2. J. Brough, "Audumbarāyaṇa's Theory of Language," in *Bulletin of the School of Oriental and African Studies* XIV, (1952), pp. 73-77.
3. See Vāk., II:143, pp. 70-71.

the sentence-meaning which is always determinative.[1] This is further evidenced when it is realized that each subsequent word in the sentence conveys its partial meaning as influenced by the partial meanings of the preceding words. In each case the meaning offered by the individual word occupies only a temporary and ultimately unreal existence. As Iyer puts it, "The fact is that the understanding of these partial meanings in the middle is only a means to an end and once the end, namely, the understanding of the sentence-meaning, is achieved, the intermediary meanings are abandoned."[2] As was the case between the phoneme and word-*sphoṭa*, the relation here is the same "*vivarta*" type of paradox. The individual words of the sentence have apparent existence only because of the prior reality of the sentence-*sphoṭa*. The latter assumes phenomenal differentiation as uttered words, because (due to *avidyā*) that is the only way we can communicate and think at the level of ordinary consciousness. For us listeners, these phenomenal words become the means by which the noumenal *sphoṭa*, intended by the speaker, bursts forth upon our cognition. Once the sentence-meaning is perceived, the partial meanings of the individual words are seen to be incomplete, erroneous, and therefore totally transcended. The *vākya-sphoṭa* is the true sentence or speech-unit, which exists behind the unreal but necessary facade of sensuous phonemes and words.[3,4] The relationship between these two levels of speech is, as was shown previously, one of the superimposition or one-sided identification, with the sentence-meaning as the ultimate real.

---

1. See Iyer, *Bhartṛhari*, p. 195.

2. *Ibid.*, p. 194.

3. See Vāk., II:437-438.

4. In this connection it is interesting to note Allen's observation that for phonetic purposes the basic linguistic unit is sometimes described as the "breath-group" (*eka-prāṇa-bhāva*), corresponding in the Vedic hymns to one line of verse. The denial of independence to the word is further stressed by the Sanskrit system of writing which takes no particular account of word division. The "pada" or "word texts," having the word-isolate as the basic unit are generally recognized as products of an artificial analysis devised by grammarians, and others for the purposes of instruction. See W. S. Allen, *Phonetics in Ancient India*, pp. 9-10.

According to Bhartṛhari, the chief characteristic of the sentence is that there is a certain completeness about its meaning. This completeness is said to occur when the purpose or intention of the speaker is conveyed to the listener. In the situation where a word may have several meanings or several different words may convey the same meaning, orderly communication is brought about by the controlling influence of the speaker's intention.[1] In effecting completeness, the intention of the speaker must operate on the level of the sentence-meaning and not on the level of the word-meanings. This essential characteristic of completeness is also described by Bhartṛhari in relation to the so-called one word sentence (see, e.g., of "Lion !" above), which is common in experience. In such situations it is clear that completeness does not depend on any particular number of words which the sentence must have, nor on any particular kind of word, such as a verb, which it must contain.[2] Whatever partial meaning or grammatical status may be attributed to the phenomenal utterance of the single word sentence, the sentence-meaning is only conveyed when, through the causality supplied by the speaker's intention, added word-meanings are mentally understood so that completeness results. In the situation where the single word utterance is a noun, which alone can express only an incomplete meaning, its utterance may be pregnant with some verbal action which is added mentally so that a complete meaning is communicated.[3] If the single word utterance is a verb then the intention of the speaker results in the mental understanding of a noun and possibly other accessory word meanings, so that completeness of meaning is perceived.[4] Regarding the psychological process required in such situations, the fundamental difference of opinion between the Kumārila and the *Sphoṭa* theorists is again clearly evidenced. Kumārila requires that the unheard words be understood by inference and be individually cognized before

1. See Vāk., II:399-402.
2. See Iyer, *Bhartṛhari*, p. 196.
3. See Vāk., II:325a. In such noumenal one-word-sei ence situations, it seems as though Bhartṛhari would accept *asti* as well as *kriyā*-type verbs as meeting the requirements for completeness. See, for example, Pillai's note 82 to this *Kārikā* offering "Here is a tree ' as an example, p. 172.
4. *Ibid.*, II:325b-326a.

the complete sentence-meaning can be understood.[1] Bhartṛhari, however, holds that when a single word (be it noun or verb) is uttered, it brings, without the inference of any other word or words, but with the help of the context or the speaker's intention, any other meaning which is required to complete it.[2] For Bhartṛhari, this completeness of the sentence-meaning is experienced, not through inference, but in the special kind of perception called *pratibhā*.

Pratibhā. *Pratibhā* is described by Bhartṛhari as the perceiving of the meaning-whole of the sentence (*vākya-sphoṭa*) in a flash of intuition.[3] It is not logical in nature, not is it capable of being directly described to others. The words used in attempting to describe this *pratibhā* to someone else can do no more than evoke in the other the conditions which will allow that *vākya-sphoṭa* (already present in his inmost self) to be revealed in the listener's own *pratibhā* experience. *Pratibhā*, therefore, is of the nature of one's inner self, but normally requires uttered word or words for its manifestation. The meaning it reveals is the complete and indivisible sentence-meaning. In the context of one word sentences *pratibhā* functions to complete the sentence-meaning by making present, in a unitary act of intuition, whatever other meaning or meanings may be required —without mentally adding any word or words to the word actually uttered.

Sphoṭa theory defines *pratibhā* as the indivisible meaning expressed by a sentence which is ingrained in each person. Chakravarti attempts to make this unique aspect of Indian thought understandable to the modern reader by describing it as follows :

> To the grammarian pratibhā is inborn intelligence; it is innate and not postnatal. Pratibhā is neither an acquisition that is sense-born nor does it result from common experience. It is called saṁskāra or bhāvanā, firmly seated in our mind and linked together with the continuous currents of knowledge flowing from previous stages of existence. Here we

1. See Vāk., II:327a.
2. *Ibid.*, II:335-6. See also Iyer's summary of this argument in *Bhartṛhari*, pp. 197-198.
3. See Vāk., II:143-145.

find the justification why pratibhā is sometimes denominated as pūrva-vāsanā (knowledge drawn from prior births). The mind has, truly, says Kālidāsa, the power of recalling the deep-rooted impressions of previous births.[1]

In this explanation it is quite clear that in logically defending his conception of *pratibhā* and *vākya-sphoṭa*, the grammarian depends upon the assumption of previous existence. Once this presupposition is accepted—as it is by virtually all schools of Indian thought—then the *Sphoṭa* view of *pratibhā* (and *vākya-sphoṭa*) seems to be both reasonable and logically consistent. Bhartṛhari's main point is that it is the use of words in sentence form that rouses this innate *pratibhā* or intelligence resulting in the revelation of knowledge.[2] Without *pratibhā* and its innate connection with the *vākya-sphoṭa*, the *ṛṣi's dhī* or direct vision of reality could not be communicated or put to ordinary use.[3] Not only is it the source of all popular word usage, but, according to Kālidāsa, *pratibhā* is that function of the mind that provides the strong guiding principle when one finds oneself in the midst of doubts as to the right course of action to follow.[4] Thus both knowledge and ultimately *mokṣa* are said to flow from *pratibhā*—the self-revelation of reality.[5] Gopinath Kaviraj suggests the teleological aspect of the *Sphoṭa* view of *pratibhā* may in some sense be comparable to the concept of instinct.[6] Indeed, Bhartṛhari illustrates and supports his view of *pratibhā* by claiming that it is naturally present in all beings, who take it as authority for their conduct.[7] Even the animals are seen to conduct themselves by it in their eating, moving, loving, nesting, vocalizing, etc.[8] For the animals, as for man, it is *pratibhā* which guides and controls practical life. Bhartṛhari concludes his discussion by delineating six different kinds of *pratibhā* according to its origination. There is *pratibhā* arising from : (1) nature (*svabhāva*), (2) action prescribed by a tradition (*caraṇa*), (3) repeated practice (*abhyāsa*),

1. See Chakravarti, *Linguistic*, pp. 113-114.
2. See Vāk., II:143.
3. *Ibid.*, II:139.
4. See Chakravarti, *Linguistic*, p. 115.
5. See Kaviraj, *Pratibhā*, p. 16.
6. *Ibid.*
7. See Vāk., II:147.
8. *Ibid.*, II:148-150.

(4) concentration of the mind (*yoga*), (5) actions done in prior lives (*adṛṣṭa*), and (6) intuition given one by the grace of a special person (*viśiṣṭopahita*).[1] As Kaviraj observes, when it comes to the psychological analysis of the manifestation of *pratibhā*, the *Sphoṭa* theorists, through their reference to antenatal dispositions, seem to open the way for an explanation in terms of Yoga "psychology."[2] This would be a fruitful undertaking in a further study.

---

1. See Vāk., II:152. See also Iyer, *Bhartṛhari*, pp. 88-90.
2. Kaviraj, *Pratibhā*, p. 18.

Chapter Seven

SPHOṬA IN RELATION TO THE LEVELS OF LANGUAGE

In the above discussion of the *vākya-sphoṭa*, it is clear that, from the *Sphoṭa* viewpoint, language may be seen to operate on at least two levels. On one level there is *pratibhā* or the intuitive flash-like understanding of the sentence-meaning as a whole. On the other level there are the uttered words of the sentence. Bhartṛhari calls the latter *vaikhari vāk* (overt or elaborated speech), while the former is aptly designated as *paśyanti vāk* (speech which through *pratibhā* sees or perceives reality).[1] Between these two levels, says Bhartṛhari there is a middle or *madhyamā vāk* corresponding to the *vākya sphoṭa* in its mental separation into sentence-meaning and a sequence of manifesting word-sounds, none of which have yet been uttered. According to Bhartṛhari, these are the three levels of language through which *śabda* or *vāk* passes whenever one speaks. *Śabda*, which is at first quite internal, is gradually externalized for the purpose of communication.[2] In this way Bhartṛhari accounts for all cognition as being necessarily identified with language, since these levels of language, span the complete continuum of cognition. This is clearly expressed in one of Bhartṛhari's basic tenets : "There is no cognition in the world in which the word does not figure. All knowledge is, as it were, intertwined with the word."[3] For Bhartṛhari there is no cognition possible without the operation of *śabda*.[4] His conception of the levels

1. See Vāk., I:142.
2. See Iyer, *Bhartṛhari*, p. 144.
3. See Vāk., I:123, p. 110.
4. A thoughtful criticism of this position has been offered by Jayanta-bhaṭṭa in his *Nyāyamañjari*. The main point of his criticism seems to be that Bhartṛhari is misled when he identifies word and consciousness and takes this so-called *Śabdabrahman* as both the efficient and the material cause of knowledge. Jayanta's argument is that words simply illuminate objects which already exist—the word is not at once the illuminator and the object, otherwise what is it that the word denotes ? Then again, says Jayanta, all cognition is not necessarily determinative nor verbal in nature. In fact, in experience we

of language seems quite logical once this presupposition is accepted. Thought at the *buddhi* or differentiated stage of word-sequences is perhaps best understood as internal speaking. And *pratibhā* or intuition may be seen as a kind of muted speaking. The point being emphasized is that for Bhartṛhari speaking is the essence of consciousness, and the means to all knowledge. And it must also be clearly understood that by "speaking," "language," or "thought" what is meant is *the conveyance of meaning*—"thinking" here does not primarily refer to concept formation, the drawing of inferences, etc., all of which would exist at the two lowest levels (*vaikhari* and *madhyamā*) only. When "meaning" is identified as intertwined with consciousness (as Bhartṛhari identifies it), this satisfies instances of *pratibhā* as well as instances of more commonplace cognition, and therefore can be held to be logically possible at all levels of *vāk*, including even the very highest (i.e., the *praṇava*).

Although the primary concern of this study is not with Bhartṛhari's metaphysical speculations, it is perhaps worthwhile to briefly outline the way in which this doctrine, i.e., "no cognition without language," along with the assumption, "all difference presupposes identity," forms the groundword for the Grammarian philosophy. The latter statement necessarily leads to an advaitism or non-dualistic "absolutism." The former statement indicates the nature the unitary absolute must possess—*śabda* and *caitanya* (consciousness) inseparably mixed together, self-evident, and revealing of all knowledge. This is *Śabdabrahman.*[1] It is mainly due to the limiting function of time (*kālaśakti*) that *Śabdabrahman*, without suffering any loss of transformation, assumes differentiation as the intuited *sphoṭa* (*pratibhā*) with its uttered words and manifested meaning.[2] As in *Advaita Vedānta*,

---

first cognize the object and only then is a word roused up and used to signify it. See G. N. Shastri, "The Doctrine of Śabdabrahman—A Criticism by Jayantabhaṭṭa," in *Indian Historical Quarterly* XV, pp. 441-453. Jayanta's position would seem to lead into an infinite regress, however, in attempting to explain why a particular word should be roused up in response to a particular object. To invoke memory only lands one in the same dilemma on step further back. At some point, it would seem, some natural fitness, or self-revelation on the part of *śabda*, seems inevitable if communication is to be logically explained.

1. *Ibid.*, I:1.
2. *Ibid.*, I:3.

the metaphysical principle of beginningless ignorance or *avidyā* is held to be the initial cause of the One manifesting itself as many. Helārāja summarizes Bhartṛhari's position as follows :

> ... Within Nescience (*avidyā*) which is the cause of the phenomenal world, there emerges, first of all, the phenomenal world (*saṁsāra*), consisting in the appearance of differentiation. Differentiation is spatial and temporal. Of the two, temporal differentiation comes first in the creation of the world. Consciousness in the form *Paśyanti* is without any sequence, but when it is associated with the *Prāṇa* principle (activity) it shines as Time, as though it had sequence ...[1]

The importance of the above metaphysical considerations for our present purpose is that it is the power of time in producing sequence in our experience of the really unitary word-consciousness that results in the division of the *sphoṭa* into word-sentences which make communication possible. It is under the power of time, therefore, that the *paśyanti* level of word-consciousness assumes the lower and progressively more differentiated levels of *madhyamā* and *vaikhari*. From the hearer's point of view the process is reversed. The word-sounds (*vaikhari*) and the inner word-meanings (*madhyamā*) are both initially cognized under the sequence of time until, with the final perception of the *vākya-sphoṭa*, the level of *paśyanti* is manifested. In this *pratibhā* state noumenal knowledge dawns, and all differentiation due to the sequence of time is transcended.

Having seen how the levels of language fit into and categorize Bhartṛhari's overall metaphysics, let us now examine each level in somewhat more detail.[2] *Vaikhari* is the most external and differentiated level in which *vāk* is commonly uttered by the speaker and heard by the hearer. It is *prāṇa* or breath that enables the organs of articulation and hearing to produce and perceive sounds in a temporal sequence. *Prāṇa* may therefore be taken as the instrumental cause of *vaikhari vāk*. The chief characteristic of *vaikhari vāk* is that it has a fully developed temporal sequence. At this level individual peculiarities of the

1. Iyer, *Bhartṛhari*, p. 123. Iyer quotes Helārāja.

2. The following summary depends mainly upon Iyer's presentation of Bhartṛhari's position in *Bhartṛhari*, pp. 144-146.

speaker (e.g., accent) are present along with the linguistically relevant parts of speech. Going further inwards, as it were, *madhyamā vāk* is the next level and its association is chiefly with the mind or intellect (*buddhi*). It is the idea or series of words as conceived by the mind after hearing or before speaking out. It may be thought of as inward speech. All the parts of speech that are linguistically relevant to the sentence are present here in a latent form. At this level a variety of manifestation is possible. The same *sphoṭa* or meaning is capable of being revealed by a variety of forms of *madhyamā*, depending on the language adopted. Although there is not full temporal sequence of the kind experienced in spoken words, word and meaning are still distinct and word order is present. Therefore, temporal sequence must also be present along with its instrumental cause *prāṇa*. Traditional *Yoga* is able to demonstrate a subtle but direct connection between breathing and cognition.[1]

The next and innermost stage is *paśyanti vāk*. *Paśyanti* is the direct experience of the *vākya-sphoṭa*—of meaning as a noumenal whole. At this level there is no distinction between the word and the meaning and there is no temporal sequence. All such phenomenal differentiations drop away with the intuition of the pure meaning in itself. Yet there is present at this level a kind of "going-out" or desire for expression. This is the *pratibhā* "instinct," referred to above, which in one sense may be said to motivate the phenomenalization into sentences and words of the *paśyanti* vision, so that communication may occur. Thus the Vedic vision or *dhi* of the *ṛṣi*, which in itself is *paśyanti*, becomes phenomenalized so that by its uttered word men might rise above their ignorance and be grasped in their cognition by the revelation of ultimate reality. Therefore, there is a sense in which *Veda* and *pratibhā* are identified as *paśyanti vāk*. Since *paśyanti* is, by definition, beyond the level of differentiated cognition, it is impossible to define it in word-sentences. It is at the level of direct intuition and therefore must finally be understood through experience. Nevertheless, there has been no dearth of speculation over the exact nature of *paśyanti* and the possibility of yet a higher level of language, i.e., *parā vāk*. Although such speculation is beyond the concern of this present

1. *Yoga sūtras*, II:53.

study — with its delimitation of *buddhi* stage, and below — it should be noticed in passing that Bhartṛhari himself could quite possibly have conceived of a fourth or *parā vāk* level. The *Vṛtti* on I:142 does quote, among numerous other passages, *Ṛgveda* I:164:45, which refers to four levels of *vāk*. Of these four three remain hidden in the cave or the inner self, only the fourth is spoken by man as his external language. In this regard, Iyer offers an interesting observation on the *Vākyapadiya* itself. He points out that a very obvious parallel seems to exist between its structure and contents, and the levels of *vāk*. The first *kāṇḍa* concentrates a great deal on *Brahman*, the undifferentiated ultimate reality, to which the *paśyanti vāk* is very near. In the second *kāṇḍa* the *vākya-sphoṭa* is the subject with its paradox of containing both the differentiation of the sentence-words and the unitary meaning at the same time. And this parallels the *madhyamā* level of *vāk*. The third *kāṇḍa* concentrates almost totally on analysis of parts of speech and their differentiation, which clearly seems identical with the realm of *vaikhari vāk*. Iyer finds support for such a parallelism from Helārāja. If this position can be taken, then the parallel to the level of *parā vāk* might well be taken as the whole of the *Vākyapadiya*. For in this work it is the indivisible whole of the speaking act, or better yet, "speech itself," which Bhartṛhari is analyzing. As Iyer observes, it is remarkable how Bhartṛhari, throughout the *Vākyapadiya*, is ever conscious of the highest word-principle, the *Śabdatattva*—"Brahman out of which the whole cosmos and our experience of it consisting of an infinite variety of cognitions, objects and words expressive of them, are manifested."[1] Another scholar, Kunjunni Raja, suggests that although later Grammarians have been influenced by the *Pratyabhijñā* School, which interprets *Śabdabrahman* as having a fourth or *parā vāk* stage of manifestation, in Bhartṛhari himself no stage higher than *paśyanti vāk* is found.[2] However, Gaurinath Sastri has made a detailed comparison between the classification of *vāk* as found in both Bhartṛhari and Kashmir *Trika* writers and concludes that the two systems do not differ significantly. Sastri points out that for Bhartṛhari the supreme reality is

1. Iyer, *Bhartṛhari*, p. 68; see also, pp. 66-67.
2. See Raja, *Theories*, p. 147.

conceived of in terms of *śabda* or *vāk* in such a way that there is no real difference between *Śabdabrahman* and *Parabrahman*—they merely represent two aspects of the same supreme *Śabda*. Consequently, *Śabda Brahman* is synonymous with *Paśyanti* and *Para Brahman* with *Parā Vāk*. According to *Trika* thought, *Parā Vāk* is given a subtle logical distinction in that it is described as a power of the supreme reality *Parama Śiva*—yet both *Parama Śiva* and his power *Parā Vāk* (or *Vimarśa*) are held to be identical in essence. Whereas for Bhartṛhari and his followers *Parā Vāk* is taken to be independent and self-subsistent, the *Trika* writers place *Parā Vāk* in a dependent relationship with *Parama Śiva*. *Parama Śiva* is described as the substantive or the powerful, while *Parā Vāk* is the attribute or the power. G. N. Sastri concludes his comparison by suggesting that Bhartṛhari's writing was earlier than that of the *Trika* writers, and that their subsequent speculations have led to a different conception of *Parā Vāk*—but a difference which is more logical than real in its nature. However, it may also be that the distinction insisted on by the *Trika* philosophers is a direct result of Bhartṛhari's equation of *paśyanti* (from the root *dṛś*—to see in the present time) with the supreme reality. "Seeing" admits a multiplicity in that relation with an object is implied, and this is clearly unacceptable as a description of the ultimate necessitating a higher level of *vāk*.[1]

The question as to whether or not Bhartṛhari intended a fourth or *parā vāk* level is a problem which at this time seems to remain unresolved. For our present purposes, however, it is not of crucial importance since we are not concerned with the more mystical metaphysical speculations. Our focus is primarily upon the more psychological aspects of the *vaikharī* and the *madhyamā* levels and the nature of the *paśyanti pratibhā* which is involved therein. Before leaving this discussion of the various levels of *vāk*, it should perhaps be noted that some other traditions have made much of these same four levels. In both Tantrism and in Kashmir Śaivism, an *advaita* or non-dualism is adopted, and the *parā vāk* level is given great speculative elaboration; yet there appears to be much in common with the

1. See Sastri, *Word*, pp. 66-82.

main tenets of Bhartṛhari's philosophy.[1] From the viewpoint of *Śaiva Siddhānta*, however, the Grammarian's interpretation is criticized in a fashion similar to the previously mentioned objection of Jayantabhaṭṭa. In the *Śaiva Siddhānta* view *śabda* is not self-revealing, but serves only to illuminate the meaning which is located in the independently existing object (*artha*).[2] Because of this basic disagreement in presupposition, the interpretation given to the four levels of *vāk*, and especially to that of *parā vāk*, is quite different from that offered by Bhartṛhari.[3] As K. Sivaraman notes, *Śaiva Siddhānta* rejects the *Śabdabrahman* position and looks on the *parā* level "not as *brahman* but as *śakti—parigraha-śakti* of *brahman* and its unfoldment into concrete and overt speech forms as a case of real change of states, modal change (*vṛtti*) not unreal appearances."[4]

Returning to Bhartṛhari's own position, we see that the very ontological reality of *vāk* throughout its various levels also amounts to a description of the path by which *mokṣa* (ultimate freedom from ignorance) may be attained. In *Vākyapadīya* I:14 we read "It (Grammar) is the door to salvation, the remedy for all the impurities of speech, the purifier of all the sciences and shines in every branch of knowledge."[5] The *vṛtti* following makes clear that use of corrupt forms of *vāk* is a cause of sin, and that the correct use of *vāk* not only reveals all knowledge but, at the same time, results in the acquiring of special merit through which one may become united with *Śabdabrahman* and eventually, by repeated repetition of this union, *mokṣa* is finally achieved. It is at the level of *paśyantī vāk* or *pratibhā* that such union, productive of *mokṣa*, is depicted. Iyer describes such a practice as *śabdapūrvayoga* or *vāgyoga* which he defines as a kind of meditation aimed at raising consciousness to the highest level of *vāk*.[6] Absence of differentiation or time sequence within the *vākyasphoṭa* is held to be characteristic of this meditation. Iyer finds

1. See Chakravarti's interpretation of the levels of *vāk*, in *Linguistic*, pp. 49-51, which he seems to base on the Tantric text "Mañjūṣā." See also John Woodroffe's presentation on the levels of *vāk* in Tantric Mantra, *The Garland of Letters*, pp. 65-76, and in *Śakti and Śākta*, Ch. 24.

2. K. Sivaraman, *Śaivism in Philosophical Perspective*, p. 229.

3. *Ibid.*, pp. 223-229.

4. *Ibid.*

5. See Vāk., p. 21.

6. Iyer, *Bhartṛhari*, p. 145.

the required discipline described in the vṛtti *Vākyapadiya* I:123 which he translates as follows :

> Taking his stand on the essence of the Word lying beyond the activity of breath (*prāṇa*), resting in one's self with all sequence eliminated,
>
> After having purified speech and after having rested it on the mind, after having broken its bonds and made it bond-free, After having reached the inner Light, he with his knots cut, becomes united with the Supreme Light.[1]

Although Bhartṛhari is emphatic that the study of the correct use and meaning of *vāk* is a means of attaining *mokṣa*, he does not describe the different stages of that spiritual ascent. As Iyer points out, Bhartṛhari seems to do little more than to observe the levels of *vāk*, particularly the *vaikharī*, *madhyamā* and *paśyantī*, and indirectly suggest that they are somehow connected with the process of ascent to *mokṣa*.[2] An analysis showing how *Sphoṭa* theory as a practical spiritual discipline could psychologically result in *mokṣa* would be an interesting and worthwhile subject in a further study.

1. Iyer, *Bhartṛhari*, p. 145.
2. *Ibid.*, p. 404.

CHAPTER EIGHT

SUMMARY AND CONCLUSION

Summary of Major Sphoṭa *Tenets*

The above philosophical analysis has examined the *Sphoṭa* theory of language as revelation for evidence of its logical possibility. This analysis has been carried out within the context of the critical dialogue between the *Sphoṭa* theorists and their most thoroughgoing critic the *Mīmāṁsaka* Kumārila Bhaṭṭa. The criterion applied throughout has been "logical possibility" with "logical" defined as "reasonably to be believed, and defensible on the grounds of consistency." As a result of this analysis, the following summary is offered of the major *Sphoṭa* tenets which are judged to have satisfied the philosophical requirement of being logically possible.

A. The primary unit of language is the *sphoṭa* or meaning-whole; its physical manifestation as a series of uttered words or phonemes is secondary.

   1. An uttered word or phoneme has no independent existence apart from the meaning-whole of which it is a part, i.e., the sentence (*vākya-sphoṭa*).

   2. The primary meaning-whole or *sphoṭa* phenomenalizes into parts (i.e., *padas* and phonemes) because there is a potentiality to burst forth into disclosure (*sphuṭ*) within the *sphoṭa* (self-revelation is the telos of language and consciousness). To put it another way, there is an inherent desire within the individual self to communicate—speech has an instinctive basis.

   3. The two aspects of word-sound (*dhvani*) and word-meaning (*artha*), differentiated in the mind (*buddhi*) and yet integrated like two sides of the same coin, constitute the *sphoṭa*.

B. Meaning is communicated, not by the summation of phonemes/*padas* or their special *apūrva* like powers, but by the progressive revelation of the inherent *vākya-sphoṭa* as the phonemes/*padas* are uttered.

1. *Sphoṭa* is an *a priori* meaning whole, which is fully perceived in the mind of the speaker before he begins to speak, and is latent in the minds of all hearers. The uttered sounds serve only to manifest to the hearer the *sphoṭa* which is already latent in his consciousness, and which is identical with the speaker's initial *sphoṭa*.
2. The manifesting of the *sphoṭa* in the cognition of the hearer is a process of perception, rather than inference. This process is characterized as a series of progressively clearer perceptions, the first having the highest degree of error, the last having no error at all.

   a. There are levels of language characterized by different degrees of phenomenalization of the *sphoṭa*.

   (1) At the lower levels of *vaikharī* and *madhyamā*, the *sphoṭa* is limited by the function of time sequence which occurs in conjunction with *prāṇa*, and results in ordinary verbal cognition—overt speech and mental thought.

   (2) At the higher level of *paśyantī*, ordinary verbal cognition is transcended and the noumenal meaning of the *vākya-sphoṭa* bursts forth in a flash of intuition or *pratibhā*.

Since the above include almost all of the major theoretical tenets proposed by Bhartṛhari, this analysis indicates that from the philosophic viewpoint at least, the *Sphoṭa* Theory of language as revelation is logically possible. However, there are two claims made by Bhartṛhari which, it is judged, have not as yet received philosophic elucidation so as to show forth their logical possibility. Consequently, they have not been included in the above summary. They are (1) The claim that the *Sphoṭa* Theory (probably via the levels of language) is a means for attaining *mokṣa*, and (2) The claim that the *śabdabhāvanā* (i.e., the residual trace of the use of words in previous lives), with which every child is born, is somehow transformed into knowledge of a particular language as the child grows up. As Iyer observes, since the *vākya-sphoṭa* are indivisible units and are the only real elements in the *Sphoṭa* view, the process by which the child learns language must be much more than merely learning the meanings of individual words by watching the usage of elders and using the method of agreement, difference and elimination, such as the *Mīmāṁsakas* suggest. But neither Bhartṛhari nor his commentators have as yet shown how a child achieves knowledge of the particular language community into which he is born. From the point of view of philosophical analysis both of these claims remain as problems for future examination and testing for evidence of their logical possibility. Some help in this direction may be forthcoming if one or both of these claims can be shown to have psychological possibility, and this will be attempted in a subsequent study.

Conclusion

The oral emphasis on the Indian approach to language has strongly shaped the kind of grammar and philosophy of language that has developed. As a major representative of this approach Bhartṛhari's *Sphoṭa* Theory of language was examined. Although very different from most modern linguistic theories, the logic of the *Sphoṭa* Theory is that the overt word sounds simply manifest or reveal, but do not create, the idea. The idea or *sphoṭa* is a given which is present in all consciousness. This resonates with ordinary experience. In talking over coffee or in writing an essay one starts with an idea which when clear in our mind creates an impulse for expression or communication. Then there is the mental struggle to break down the idea or *sphoṭa* into words and sentences. But no matter how hard one tries the whole of the original idea can never be pressed out into words. Something always remains leftover and unsaid. If meaning were communicated by conveying or passing the actual meaning from one to another, then meaning would constantly be being lost and eventually language would cease to communicate. In Bhartṛhari's view, however, communication is possible only because language and its meaning is grounded in a common consciousness which is Divine in nature.

While not all may agree with the Indian approach in general or with Bhartṛhari in particular, it is a view of language which makes sense of poetry, revealed scripture, science, the mystical changing of *mantras*, and in addition, strongly resonates with our ordinary everyday experience of coffee-cup chat. It is a way of seeing language which effectively explains why it is that sometimes when we listen we do not hear. It also teaches how to remove the obstructions in one's consciousness so that real hearing becomes possible, and suggests that "In the beginning was God, and the Word was with God, and the Word was God" is the ultimate wisdom to be heard.

BIBLIOGRAPHY

1. *Primary Sources*

Bhagavadgītā, trans. by W. D. P. Hill. Oxford : Oxford University Press, 1966.

Brahmasiddhi of Maṇḍana Miśra, edited with introduction by S. Kuppuswami Sastri. Madras : Government Press, 1937.

Brahma-Sūtra-Śāṅkara-Bhāṣya, trans. by V. M. Apte. Bombay : Popular Book Depot, 1960.

Māṇḍūkyopaniṣad, The, trans. by Swāmī Nikhilānanda. Mysore : Sri Ramakrishna Ashrama, 1936.

Pañcadaśi of Vidyāraṇya, trans. by Swami Swahananda, Madras: Sri Ramakrishna Math, 1967.

Pañcapādikā of Padmapāda, trans. by D. Venkataramiah, Baroda: Oriental Institute, 1948.

Rasādhyāya of the Nāṭyaśāstra, trans. by J. L. Mason and M. V. Patwardhan, Poona : Deccan College, Vols. I & II, 1970.

Śābdanirṇaya by Prakāśātmayatindra, edited by T. Ganapati Shastri. Trivandrum: Government Press, 1917. "Trivandrum Sanskrit Series", No. LIII.

Sāṁkhya Aphorisms of Kapila, trans. by J. R. Ballantyne. Varanasi: Chowkhamba Sanskrit Series, 4th ed., 1963.

Sāṅkhya Kārikā of Īśvara Kriṣṇa, trans. by H. T. Colebrooke, with the *Bhāṣya of Gauḍapāda*. Oxford: A. J. Valpy, 1837.

Sāṅkhya Kārikā of Īśvara Kriṣṇa, trans. by J. Davies. Calcutta: Susil Gupta, 2nd ed., 1947.

Sarva-Darśana-Saṁgraha by Mādhava, trans. by E. B. Cowell and A. E. Gough. (London: Kegan Paul, Trench, Trubner), Varanasi: Chowkhamba Sanskrit Series Reprint, 1961.

Ślokavārttika by Kumārilabhaṭṭa, trans. by Ganganatha Jha. Calcutta : Asiatic Society of Bengal, 1909.

Sphoṭavāda of Nāgeśa Bhaṭṭa, ed. by V. V. Krishnamacharya. Madras : The Theosophical Society, 1946.

Sphoṭasiddhi of Maṇḍana Miśra, trans. by K. A. S. Iyer. Poona : Deccan College, 1966.

Tattvabindu of Vācaspati Miśra, edition critique traduction et introduction par Madelein Biardeau. Pondichery : Institut Francais d'Indologie, 1956.

Principal Upanisads, The, trans. by S. Radhakrishnan. London: Allen and Unwin Ltd., 1962.

Thirteen Principal Upanisads, The, trans. by R. E. Hume. Oxford: Oxford University Press, 1965.

Vākyapadīya of Bhartṛhari with the Commentaries *Vṛtti* and *Paddhati* of Vṛṣabhadeva, edited by K. A. Subramania Iyer. Poona : Deccan College, 1966.

Vākyapadīya of Bhartṛhari with the *Vṛtti*, trans. by K. A. Subramania Iyer. Poona: Deccan College, Ch. I (1965) and Ch. III, Pt. i (1971).

Vākyapadīya of Bhartṛhari, trans. by K. A. S. Iyer. Delhi: Motilal Banarsidass, Ch. III, pt. ii, 1974: and Ch. II, 1977.

Vākyapadīya, The, edited with trans. by K. Raghavan Pillai. Varanasi : Motilal Banarsidass, Cantos I and II, 1971.

Vedānta Paribhāṣā of Dharmarāja Adhvarin, trans. by S. S. Sastri. Adyar : Adyar Library and Research Center, 1942.

Vedānta Sūtras, The, with the *Commentary* by Śaṅkara, trans. by G. Thibaut. Delhi : Motilal Banarsidass, 1962. (Reprint of "Sacred Books of the East," Vol. 34, 1904.)

Vyākaraṇa-Mahābhāṣya of Patañjali, edited by S. D. Joshi. Poona: University of Poona, 1968.

Yogadarśanam of Patañjali, Varanasi : Bhāratīya Vidyā Prakāśana, 1963.

Yoga System of Patañjali, The, with the *Bhāṣya* of Vyāsa and the *Ṭīkā* of Vācaspati Miśra, trans. by J. H. Woods. Delhi: Motilal Banarsidass 1966. (Reprint of "Harvard Oriental Series," Vol. 17, 1914.)

Yoga Sūtras of Patañjali, trans. by Rama Prasada. Delhi: Oriental Books Reprint Corporation, 1978.

2. *Secondary Sources*

Ajñāna : The Theory of Ignorance, by Malkani, Das and Murti. London : Luzac and Co., 1933.

Allen, W. S., *Phonetics in Ancient India* : London: Oxford University Press, 1953.

Apte, V. S., *The Practical Sanskrit-English Dictionary*, Delhi: Motilal Banarsidass, 1965, 3rd ed.

Arapura, J. G., "Language and Phenomena." *Canadian Journal of Theology* 15 (1970), 41-53.

——, *Religion as Anxiety and Tranquility*. The Hague : Mouton, 1972.

Bhatt, Govardhan, P. *Epistemology of the Bhāṭṭa School of Pūrva Mīmāṁsā*. Varanasi : Chowkhamba Sanskrit Series, 1962.

Biardeau, M. *Théorie de la Connaissance et Philosophie de la Parole* Paris : Mouton, 1964.

Brough, J. "Audumbarāyaṇa's Theory of Language." *Bulletin of the School of Oriental and African Studies* 14 (1952), 73-77.

Cassirer, E. *An Essay on Man*. Toronto: Bantam Books, 1970.

——, *Language and Myth*, trans. by S. K. Langer. New York : Dover Publications, 1953.

Chakrabarti, Tarapada. *Indian Aesthetics and Science of Language*. Calcutta : Sanskrit Pustak Bhandar, 1971.

Chakravarti, P. K., *The Linguistic Speculations of the Hindus*. Calcutta : University of Calcutta, 1933.

——, *The Philosophy of Sanskrit Grammar*. Calcutta : University of Calcutta, 1930.

Chari, V. K. "Rasa as an Aesthetic Concept: Some Comments from the Point of view of Western Criticism," Unpublished Paper, International Sanskrit Conference, March, 1972, New Delhi.

——, "Poetic Emotions and Poetic Semantics", *Journal of Aesthetics and Art Criticism*, 24, (1976), 287-299.

Chaterjee, Satischandra. *The Nyāya Theory of Knowledge*. Calcutta : University of Calcutta, 1965.

Chatterjee, S. C., and Datta, D. M., *An Introduction to Indian Philosophy*. Calcutta : University of Calcutta, 1939.

Chomsky, N:, *Language and Mind*. New York : Harcourt, Brace and World Inc., 1968.

Collected Papers of Professor S. S. Suryanarayana Sastri, ed. by T. M. P. Mahadevan. Madras : University of Madras, 1961.

Coward, Harold G., *Bhartṛhari*, Boston : G. K. Hall, 1976.

——, and Sivaraman, Krishna. *Revelation in Indian Thought* A Festschrift in honour of Professor T. R. V. Murti, Emeryville, California : Dharma Publishing, 1977.

——, (ed.) "*Language*" *in Indian Philosophy and Religion*. Waterloo : Wilfrid Laurier University Press, 1978.

Dasgupta, S., *A History of Indian Philosophy*. Cambridge : University Press, 1963, Vol. 1.

——, Yoga Philosophy, Calcutta : University of Calcutta, 1930.

Datta, D. M., *The Six Ways of Knowing*. Calcutta : University of Calcutta, 1960.

Deussen, P., *The Philosophy of the Upanisads*. New York : Dover Pub. Inc., 1966.

——, *The System of Vedānta*. Chicago : The Open Court Pub. Co., 1912.

Devasthali, G. V., *Mīmāṁsā : The Vākya-Śāstra of Ancient India*. Bombay : Booksellers' Pub. Co., 1959.

Fraser, R. *The Language of Adam*. New York: Columbia University Press, 1977.

Ghose, Aurobindo, *On the Veda*. Pondichery : Sri Aurobindo Ashram Press, 1956.

Gonda, J., *The Vision of the Vedic Poets*. The Hague : Mouton & Co., 1963.

Godamer, Hans-Georg, *Philosophical Hermeneutics*, trans. by D. E. Linge, Berkley : University of California Press, 1976.

Handbook of Christian Theology, ed. by M. Halverson and A. Cohen. New York : World Publishing Co., 1958.

Herman, A. L., "Sphoṭa," *Journal of the Ganganatha Jha Research Institute* 19 (1963), 1-21.

Iyer, Subramania K. A., *Bhartrhari*. Poona: Deccan College, 1969.

——, "The Conception of Guṇa Among the Vaiyākaraṇas", *New Indian Antiquary* 5 (6), 121-130.

——, "The Doctrine of Sphoṭa," *Journal of the Ganganatha Jha Research Institute* 5, 121-147.

Jayatilleke, K. N., *Early Buddhist Theory of Knowledge*. London: Allen and Unwin Ltd., 1963.

Jha, Ganganatha, *Pūrva-Mīmāṁsā in its Sources*. Varanasi : Banaras Hindu University, 2nd ed., 1964.

Joshi, S. D., "Patañjali's Definition of a Word—An Interpretation," *Bulletin of the Deccan College Research Institute* 25 (1966), 65-70.

Kaviraj, Gopinath, "The Doctrine of Pratibhā in Indian Philosophy", *Annals of the Bhandarkar Oriental Research Institute*, 1924, pp. 1-18 and 113-132.

Larson, G. J., *Classical Sāṁkhya*. Delhi : Motilal Banarsidass, 1969.

Mahadevan, T. M. P., *The Philosophy of Advaita*. London : Luzac & Co., 1938.

McArthur, H., *In Search of the Historical Jesus*, New York : Charles Scribners, 1969.

Matilal, B. K., *Epistemology, Logic and Grammar in Indian Philosophical Analysis*. The Hague : Mouton, 1971.

Mehta, M. L., *Outlines of Jaina Philosophy*. Bangalore : Jaina Mission Society, 1954.

Monier-Williams, M., *A Sanskrit-English Dictionary*. Oxford : Clarendon Press, 1956.

Murti, T. R. V., *The Central Philosophy of Buddhism*. London : Allen and Unwin Ltd., 1960.

——, "Some Comments on the Philosophy of Language in the Indian Context," *Journal of Indian Philosophy*, 2, (1974), 321-331.

Murty, K. S., *Revelation and Reason in Advaita Vedānta*. New York : Columbia University Press, 1959.

Muller, Max K. M., *Lectures on the Science of Language*. Delhi : Munshi Ram Manohar Lal (1861), reprint, 1965.

——, *The Six Systems of Indian Philosophy*. London : Longmans, Green and Co., 1919.

Northrop, F. S. C., *The Logic of the Sciences and the Humanities*. New York : MacMillan Co., 1947.

Oxford Annotated Bible, R. S. V., The, ed. by H. G. May and B. M. Metzger. New York : Oxford University Press, 1962.

Pandey, K. C., *Abhinavagupta*. Varanasi : Chowkhamba Sanskrit Series Office, 1963.

Pandeya, R. C., *The Problem of Meaning in Indian Philosophy*. Delhi : Motilal Banarsidass, 1963.

Piaget, J. *Insights and Illusions of Philosophy*, trans. by W. Mays. New York : The World Publishing Co., 1971.

Potter, K. H., *Presuppositions of India's Philosophies*. New Delhi : Prentice-Hall of India, Ltd., 1965.

Radhakrishnan, S., *Indian Philosophy*. London : Allen and Unwin, Ltd., 1962, Vol. I.

Radhakrishnan, S. and Moore, C. A., *A Source Book in Indian Philosophy*. Princeton : Princeton University Press, 1967.

Raghavan, V., *Bhoja's Śṛṅgāra Prakāśa*. Madras : The Theosophical Society, 1963.

——, *Some Concepts of Alaṃkāra Śāstra*. Adyar : Theosophical Publishing House, 1942.

Raja, K. Kunjunni, *Indian Theories of Meaning*. Adyar : Adyar Library and Research Center, 1963.

Ranade, R. D., *A Constructive Survey of Upanisadic Philosophy*. Bombay : Bharatiya Vidya Bhavan, 1968 (1926).

Religious Experience and Truth, ed. by S. Hook. New York : New York University Press, 1961.

Republic of Plato, The, trans. by Allan Bloom. New York : Basic Books Inc., 1968.

Riepe, D., *The Naturalistic Tradition in Indian Thought*. Seattle : University of Washington Press, 1961.

Sapir, Edward, *Language*. New York : Harcourt Brace and World, 1949.

Sastri, D. N., *Critique of Indian Realism*. Agra University, 1964.

Sastri, G. N., "The Doctrine of Śabdabrahman—A Criticism by Jayantabhaṭṭa," *Indian Historical Quarterly* 15 (1939), 441-453

Sastri, Gaurinath, *The Philosophy of Word and Meaning*. Calcutta : Sanskrit College, 1959.

Sastri, P. S., Subrahmanya, *Lectures on Patañjali's Mahābhāṣya*. Thiruvaiyaru, 1960, Vol. I, 2nd ed.

Savitri, Sister, "The Power of the Divine Word", *Vedānta Kesari* 47 (1960-61), 395-398.

Sen-Gupta, Anima, *Classical Sāṁkhya : A Critical Study*. Patna : University Press, 1969.

Shakespeare, William, *The Works of* ... London : Frederick Warne and Co., 1893.

Sinha, J., *Indian Psychology : Cognition*. Calcutta : Sinha Publishing House, 1958.

Sivaraman, K., *Śaivism in Philosophical Perspective*. Varanasi : Motilal Banarsidass, 1972.

Staal, J. F. (ed.) *A Reader on the Sanskrit Grammarians*, Cambridge: MIT Press, 1972.

———, "The Concept of Metalanguage and Its Indian Background", *The Journal of Indian Philosophy*, 3, 1975, pp. 315-354.

Tatia, Nathmal, *Studies in Jaina Philosophy*. Banaras : Jaina Cultural Research Society, 1951.

Tripathi, R. K., "The Unspeakable in Metaphysics" in *Revelation in Indian Thought*, ed. by H. G. Coward and K. Sivaraman. Emeryville : Dharma Publishing, 1977, pp.171-183.

Urbanm, W. M., *Language and Reality*. London : George Allen and Unwin Ltd., 1951.

Varma, Satyakam, *Studies in Indology*. Delhi : Bharatiya Prakashan, 1976.

Von Humboldt, Wilhelm, *Linguistic Variability and Intellectual Development*, trans. by G. C. Buck and F. A. Raven.

Wittgenstein, L., *Tractatus Logico-Philosophicus*, with trans. to English by D. F. Pears and B. F. McGuiness. London : Routledge and Kegan Paul, 1961.

Woodroffe, J., *The Garland of Letters : Studies in the Mantra Śāstra.*

——, *Śakti and Śākta*. Madras : Ganesh and Co., 1965.

Zimmer, H., *Philosophies of India*. Princeton: Princeton University Press, 1969.

GLOSSARY OF SANSKRIT TERMS

abhidhā, primary meaning.

abhiniveśa, clinging to life.

abhyāsā, habitual steadying of the mind in Yogic concentration.

adhyāsā, superimposition.

āgama, scriptural truth, including *śruti*, *smṛti*, the epics and Purāṇas.

ahaṁkāra, ego.

ahiṁsā, non-violence in thought and deed.

akliṣṭa, unafflicted, pure, free from ignorance.

ālambana, supporting object, ground.

alaṁkāra, figure of speech.

antaḥkaraṇa, the internal mental organ composed of the *buddhi*, *ahaṁkāra*, and *manas* functions.

anumāna, inference.

aparigraha, absence of avarice.

apauruṣeya, used to indicate that Vedic scripture is authorless, eternal, and therefore safeguarded from error.

apūrva, special force or residual effect of a religious sacrificial act that inheres in the sacrificer as a special kind of potency until it brings the reward of heaven.

artha, word-meaning as distinct from word-sound; the inner meaning of a word; object.

āsana, Yogic posture for the purpose of immobilizing the body, e.g., lotus position.

asmitā, egoity.

asteya, nonstealing.

ātman, self or soul.

AUM, the sacred syllable of Hinduism that symbolizes and evokes all levels of consciousness, all knowledge of the Divine.

avidyā, the obscuring veil of human ignorance that, when removed, reveals knowledge of reality.

bhāṣya, commentary.

bīja, seed or seed state.

brahmacarya, celibacy in thought and action.

Brahman, the Absolute; the Divine; sometimes characterized as pure consciousness.

Brahma Sūtra, a summary and exposition of the basic teachings of the Upaniṣads from the viewpoint of the Vedānta School of philosophy. It is said to have been composed by Bādarāyaṇa about the second century B.C. Important commentaries on the *Brahma Sūtra* have been written by Śaṅkara and Rāmānuja.

buddhi, the level of consciousness characterized by intelligent discrimination; intellect.

buddhitattva, pure collective or universal consciousness containing within it all intellects of individuals.

citta, consciousness including both the level of awareness and the level of unconsciousness.

citta vṛtti, a particular mental state.

darśana, viewpoint; philosophical school.

dhāraṇā, short Yogic concentration with momentary loss of subject-object duality.

dharma, one's religious and moral duty in life; doing one's *dharma* produces spiritual merit; also may mean truth.

dhvani, the physical sound or the uttered syllables of a word.

dhvani (in Indian aesthetics), the use of poetic or dramatic words to suggest or evoke a feeling that is too deep, intense, and universal to be spoken.

dhyāna, Yogic concentration lasting several *dhāraṇās*; the uninterrupted flow of fixed concentration upon an *artha*, or object.

dveṣa, disgust.

guṇa, a characteristic or quality; usually refers to the three *guṇas* of consciousness : *sattva*, *rajas*, and *tamas*.

guru, spiritual teacher.

Īśvara, in the Yoga view is the divine *guru* of the ancient *ṛṣis*; it is the Divine Word of the scripture in its transcendental essence that makes up the pure consciousness of *Īśvara*.

Īśvarapranidhāna, offering up of all action and thought to the Lord Īśvara.

jīva, the empirical self, individual being.

jñāna, true, unobscured knowledge of the word or object.

kaivalya, the Sāṅkhya term for release; the *puruṣa* fully revealed in its isolated splendour.

kārikā, a concise verse requiring an interpretative commentary for its understanding.

karma, the trace or seed left behind by each thought or action that predisposes one to a similar thought or action in the future.

kleśas, constantly changing painful states of consciousness.

kliṣṭa, afflicted by ignorance.

kratu, an energy (within the word) that seeks to burst forth into expression; the drive to diversity within the unitary whole, or ***sphoṭa***.

lakṣaṇa, secondary meaning.

madhyamā vāk, language as thought that has not yet been uttered.

mahāvākyas, the great criterion sentences of the Upaniṣads, e.g. : "That thou art."

manas, the mental organ that collects and co-ordinates information.

mantra, a verse of poetic scripture in praise of the Divine.

māyā, the illusion of the manifold world, which is really only the unitary Absolute; for Śaṅkara, has the ontological status of being neither real nor unreal but inexpressible.

Mīmāṁsā, one of the six orthodox schools of Indian philosophy, argues for the authorlessness and eternality of the letter sounds of the Vedas.

mokṣa, release, freedom from the suffering and bondage of this world, oneness with the Divine.

nāda, physical sound.

nirvāṇa, Buddhist state of release or enlightenment.

nirvicāra, a pure form of ***samādhi*** in which the meaning or object is fully revealed in its very essence. No notions of time, space, or causality are present.

Nirvitarka, trance concentration upon the gross form of the object, but freed from the confusion of memory and the conventional use of words.

niyamas, positive Yogic practices for the purifying of body and mind.

Parama Śiva, Śiva as the Absolute Lord upon which the ***parā vāk*** of Kashmir is dependent.

parā vāk, an ultimate or fourth level of language developed by Kashmir Śaiva writers.

paśyantī vāk, level of intuitive or flashlike understanding of the sentence meaning as a whole.

prajñā, direct intuitive knowledge of things as they are in themselves, rather than as they appear to us.

prakṛti, non-intelligent matter, one side of the Sāṅkhya-Yoga metaphysical duality.

pramā, true cognition or knowing as distinct from false knowing.

pramāṇa, a true or valid way of knowing, e.g,; perception. Although there is argument in Indian philosophy, six *pramāṇas* are often discussed: perception, inference, analogy, presumption, nonapprehension (*abhāva*), and the revelatory power of speech (*śabda*). It is with the *pramāṇa* of *śabda* that Bhartṛhari is most concerned.

prāṇa, breath; the instrumental cause of speech at the lower levels of language.

praṇava, AUM, the sacred "root" sound from which all language flows forth.

prāṇāyāma, regulation of respiration.

pratibhā, immediate supersensuous intuition; supernormal perception that transcends the ordinary categories of time, space, and causality, and has the capacity to directly "grasp" the real nature of things.

pratyāhāra, withdrawal of senses from worldly attachments.

pratyaya, ground or support in which the word-sound and word-meaning inhere.

puruṣa, an individual pure consciousness, one side of the Sāṅkhya-Yoga metaphysical duality.

rāga, passion.

rajas, the aspect of consciousness that is passion or energy.

rasa, a dominant mood evoked in the aesthetic experience of poetry and drama.

rasadhvani, the inner essence of the aesthetic experience that is beyond all conceptual expression.

rīti, poetic style.

ṛṣi, an original seer or "speaker" of Hindu scripture. One who has purged himself of all ignorance, rendering his consciousness transparent to the Divine Word.

śabda, word or words that when spoken convey knowledge—especially of the Divine.

Śabdabrahman, the Absolute, the Divine for Bhartṛhari; the intertwined unity of word and consciousness that is the one ultimate reality; for Bhartṛhari both the material and efficient cause of creation; also called the Divine Word. or *Daivī-Vāk*.

śabdapūrvayoga, the spiritual discipline of meditating upon the Divine Word, leads to *mokṣa*, or release.

Śabdatattva, Brahman as the omniscient word-principle.

sādhanā, a personal discipline or practice for spiritual self-realization.

samādhi, trance state of consciousness with no subject-object distinction.

samprajñāta samādhi, "seeded" or trance concentration upon an object, as opposed to "unseeded" or trance concentration without an object.

saṁsāra, rebirth in the suffering and bondage of this world; the continual round of birth-death-rebirth; the world of phenomena.

saṁskāra, a memory trace that has the dynamic quality of a seed that is constantly ready to sprout.

saṁtoṣa, contentment.

saṅketa, convention of language usage as maintained by the elders in this and previous generations.

Sāṅkhya, one of the six orthodox schools of Indian philosophy, argues for a dualism of matter (*prakṛti*) and individual souls (*puruṣas*).

śānta rasa, the aesthetic experience of spiritual serenity; the absolute *rasa* into which all other emotions subside.

śāstra, authoritative teaching.

sattva, the aspect of consciousness that is brightness or intelligence.

sattva saṁskāra, series, continuous flow of pure consciousness as it would be in the mind of the Lord (Īśvara); no distinction between word and meaning, but only the constant presence of meaning as a whole.

satya, truthfulness.

savicāra, a form of *samādhi* in which little error is present; the intensity of concentration produces transparent *sattva* so that the true meaning or object (*artha*) stands revealed with only slight distortions of time, space, and causality.

savitarka, indistinct Yogic concentration or *samādhi* in which memory, word, and object are indiscriminately mixed together.

sāyuja, the highest spiritual goal of union with the Divine.

smṛti, secondary scripture, that which has been remembered, e.g., *Bhagavad-Gītā*.

sphoṭa, a meaning-whole or idea that eternally exists within consciousness and that is evoked or manifested by the spoken words of sentences; can be directly perceived through intuition.

śruti, primary scripture; that which has been seen by the *ṛṣis*; includes the Vedic hymns, Brāhmaṇas, and Upaniṣads.

sthayibhavas, basic dominant moods inherent in every psyche at birth.

svādhyāya, concentrated scriptural study including both meditation upon verses and chanting of AUM.

svarga, not the final release or goal of Hinduism, but the place where the fruits of the spiritual merit one has achieved are enjoyed; heaven.

tamas, the aspect of consciousness that is dullness or inertia.

tanmātras, subtle primary elements; inner counterparts to the gross sense experiences of sound, touch, colour or shape, flavour, smell.

tapas, psychic heat or energy generated from the practice of austerities; bearing with equanimity the pairs of opposites such as heat and cold, hunger and thirst.

vāgyoga, Yoga or concentration upon speech.

vaikharī vāk, gross or physical level of uttered speech.

vairāgya, turning away of the mind from all forms of worldly attachment.

vāk, language that is thought of as having various levels—from the gross form of the spoken word to the subtle form of the highest intuition.

vākya sphoṭa, intuitive understanding or direct perception of the sentence meaning as a whole idea.

varṇa, letter sounds.

vāsanā, a habit pattern of thought and/or action; composed of reinforced *karmas*.

Vedānta, one of the six orthodox schools of Indian philosophy, often identified with the monistic absolutism of Śaṅkara.

Vedas, the primary Hindu scriptures including the early hymns, the Brāhmaṇas, and Upaniṣads. The Vedas are organized into four collections called *Ṛg*, *Sāma*, *Yajur*, and *Atharva*.

vikalpa, the mixing or superimposing of two or more mental states so that knowledge is obscured and error produced.

vṛtti, a commentary.

Vyākaraṇa, the Grammar school; one of the traditional schools of Indian philosophy; Patañjali and Bhartṛhari are among the leaders of this school.

vyañjanā, special suggestive function of poetic phrases.

yamas, Yogic practices of self-restraint, e.g., *ahiṁsā*, or nonviolence.

Yoga, one of the six schools of orthodox Indian philosophy; describes a practical psychological discipline for achieving release; systematized by Patañjali.

yogāṅgas, steps or aids to the practice of Yoga.

INDEX